Mobile Pet Grooming

The Most Comprehensive Guide to Starting and Maintaining a Successful Business

Jodi Murphy
NCMG, MPS Meritus

Jodi Murphy Enterprises, LLC
PO Box 598
Stanhope, NJ 07874

Copyright ©2011 Jodi Murphy

ISBN: 978-0-9839720-0-6

All rights reserved. No part of this book may be reproduced or transmitted in any form or by any means, electronic or mechanical, including photocopying, recording, or by any information storage and retrieval system, without permission in writing from the Publisher.

All product names and brand names discussed in this book are trade names, trademarks or registered trademarks of their respective owners.

Photographs by Jodi Murphy, Danelle German and Wag'n Tails

Printed in the United States of America

The information in this book is based upon experiences and the opinion of the author. Techniques and procedures discussed within this book are only to be utilized by experienced professional groomers. We are not responsible for misuse of tools, products and/or equipment causing injury to any pet.

Book Interior Design by www.KarrieRoss.com
Book Cover Design by www.supradesign.net

A Special Thanks....

To Dave, my best friend, significant other and confidant for inspiring me to write this book. He is always there to give me the strength to reach my goals and accomplishments in life. He is my rock.

To Danelle German, for her special chapter on grooming cats in a mobile unit and for her guidance.

To Stephen Mart, for all his words of wisdom and moral support over the years.

To all the mobile groomers that expressed their passion on page 137.

To all my favorite companies and manufacturers that have brought quality equipment and supplies to this industry. Thank you all for your support.

This book is my first experience as an author. I've done my best to pour everything that I know as a professional mobile groomer into this book in hopes that I will inspire you, the reader, to go "down this road" to success.

About the Author

Jodi Murphy I have been an animal lover my entire life growing up with poodles and pointers from a very young age. My mom loved her toy poodles and my dad was an avid bird hunter, so he always had at least three pointers at one given time. I remember going to field trials as a child and found it fascinating to watch the pointers hunt. My dad loved to work his dogs in the field and still does. I was the youngest of three children and the only one who took after my dad and his love for animals, but it wasn't until later in life that the idea of grooming ever crossed my mind.

In 1995 my family was transferred to Dallas. I had two cocker spaniels at the time and was having trouble finding a groomer in the area. My dogs had the same groomer their entire life in New Jersey and they were having a hard time adjusting to the change. I finally became so frustrated with their grooming experiences that I called a local shop to see where I could go for training. I was told that I could apprentice under them; however, I would have to work as a bather for a year first. I worked on Saturdays as a bather for three groomers. After a year of bathing/brushing I apprenticed for three months.

After the first year of grooming I attended my first trade show at Groom and Kennel Expo in Pasadena. I was in awe of what was going on at the show; it was a world that I didn't even realize existed. Once I walked into the contest ring area I just sat in amazement. I knew that this was for me and boy, was I hooked. As I walked outside and saw the mobile vans I thought to myself "what a great way for me to groom around my three young children's schedules!" I ordered my new van right then and there!! The entire way home from the show I was just ecstatic and couldn't wait to start my new business.

I was the only mobile groomer in the area and my business took off like wildfire. My business was completely full within three or four months. I was very eager to learn as much as I could to bring the best service to my clients, so I started going to local dog shows to educate myself on breed profiles. I just couldn't help but to be drawn to the American Cocker Spaniels while I was there. They were sitting so beautifully with the most gorgeous long flowing coats. My jaw just dropped and at that point I knew I just had to have a puppy. The breeders who I met helped me with the grooming and got me off to the right start. One year later I entered my first grooming competition in Colorado and won Best In Show.

I began competing with other breeds, and within three years of stepping into the contest ring I was ranked third in the USA recognized by Groom Team USA. The second year on Groom Team I was ranked the #1 groomer in the USA. I traveled with Groom Team USA to Barcelona, Spain, in 2003, where I won a Gold and a Bronze medal. In 2007 I traveled again with Groom Team to Milan, Italy, where I won another Gold medal with my American Cocker Spaniel. Those are experiences that I will never forget.

In 2005 and 2006 I was awarded Best American Groomer at Intergroom in New Jersey. In 2005 I won the World Grand Champion title in the Oster Invitational Tournament of Champions. This competition was by invitation only where I competed against 42 top groomers from around the world!

After being in business for four years in Texas my family was relocated to Ohio and I had to close the business and start all over again. Once I arrived in Cincinnati, again I was the only mobile groomer in the area. Being the only mobile groomer in the area brings on its own set of challenges. Pet owners are not familiar with the higher prices that are associated with mobile grooming, which means that we must really sell ourselves and our services. When there are many mobile groomers already established in the area, be rest assured that they have set the tone when it comes to pricing.

In Cincinnati, I looked back at all the mistakes that I made in Dallas and made some changes in my pricing, routing and scheduling. It took about six months to develop my clientele base. My business did very well in Cincinnati; however, after only two years I decided to move back to my home state of New Jersey. This time around I knew that my new business in New Jersey would be "textbook." The benefit from the moves that I made over the years was that I was able to learn from my mistakes and start my new business with changes.

My business in New Jersey became equally successful in a very short period of time. I no longer have a phone number on my vehicle nor do I leave my business cards anywhere. In fact, my veterinarians' office will often ask if I am taking on new clients.

Going back to 2003, I began to work with the Andis Clipper Company as a National Grooming Consultant. I was really enjoying meeting groomers from all over the United States and noticed how eager they were to learn. I looked back at how difficult it was for me to learn, as I only had basic training through the apprenticeship program. My more advanced training came from attending seminars, from working with breeders and from the competition ring. Educating groomers was becoming a passion of mine. I found it extremely rewarding and soon realized the next step for me was to produce an instructional DVD series to help educate our industry.

In 2007 my DVD series was released. After starting out with a few DVDs on technique, I soon realized how much more I wanted it to be. I have now produced 38 titles, with so many more to come, to help groomers become the best that they can be. My DVDs have not only helped the newbie groomers get started but also have taught experienced groomers correct breed profiles and techniques. DVDs are a fabulous way to learn. You can take them to work, take them on airplanes, watch them in your mobile van and create a library for many years to come. It's one-on-one training in the privacy of your own environment. I have achieved my master certification title with two of our industry's organizations. I am a National Certified Master Groomer and Certifier for the National Dog Groomers Association of America as well as a Master Pet Stylist, Meritus with the International Society of Canine Cosmetology.

I hope you enjoy this book and that it helps you to start and run a successful mobile grooming business.

Feel free to contact me through my website, www.jodimurphy.net, if you have any questions or concerns.

Best of luck to you!

Jodi

Introduction

This book was written to inspire new groomers and seasoned groomers who are interested in starting their own mobile grooming business. The pet grooming industry has always prevailed through hard economic times for decades and decades. Pet owners consider their pets a part of their family and will spend thousands of dollars a year on proper vet care, day care, pet sitting services, quality pet food, special diets, pet insurance and grooming services for their pets.

Mobile grooming has always been in great demand. Ask any mobile groomers and they will tell you that they rarely take on new customers. This is one business that will grow quickly right before your eyes. It is human nature to be a little apprehensive about starting a new business; however, I always try to encourage new groomers to educate themselves so they will succeed. I have started three businesses in three different parts of the country and have been extremely successful with each and every one. I am very passionate about mobile grooming, and have learned so much over the years through trial and error. I will discuss with you all the do's and don'ts, so you will not make the mistakes that I made. I want to share with you my experiences—the good, the bad and the ugly—so you can learn from them.

Mobile grooming brings a very different experience for pets. They do so well when they know they are home and their family is just a hop, a skip and a jump away. Pets respond very well to peace and quiet, no distractions, no other animals and one groomer.

Mobile conversion companies have designed their vehicles with state-of-the-art technology as well as equipment. These vehicles are self contained and are completely equipped with a high velocity (HV) dryer, grooming table, vacuum, hot water heater, fresh and grey water tanks, and so on. They offer upgrades which include Clippervac systems, stereo, TV, and bathing systems. Some of the larger vehicles are equipped with bathrooms. They are truly "a salon on wheels." The most attractive benefit of mobile grooming is the flexibility and freedom that you will have when working in a mobile unit.

This book will outline every topic that you need to know about starting, running and maintaining your mobile grooming business. Maintaining and continuously fine-tuning your business is important. Following this book carefully will help you make the right decisions, preventing you from making mistakes with your vehicle and mistakes with your clients. It will also help you to become an efficient groomer. I will share with you my thoughts on equipment and tips that will help you with your grooming skills. The dogs that I groom are in stylish trims and are all on 4 to 6 week schedules with very few shave-downs. My experience in the competition ring has not only taught me how to work in an efficient manner but has also brought my skill level to the highest standards. Becoming one of the top groomers in the country has helped me to be one of the most sought-after mobile groomers in my area.

Mobile grooming is my calling and I knew from the moment that I laid eyes on the vans at a trade show that this was for me. I had no doubt that I would succeed and feel very blessed to be in this industry. It has brought so much enjoyment to my life, and I hope you will enjoy it as well.

Table of Contents

CHAPTER ONE
Business Plan 15

CHAPTER TWO
Making the Right Decision 17

CHAPTER THREE
Conversion Vehicles 21
    Choosing a Vehicle 21
    Generators vs. Inverters 26
    Propane vs. Electric 29

CHAPTER FOUR
Getting Started 31
    Vehicle Registration 31
    Insurance 31
    Registering a Business Name 31
    Zoning 32
    Overhead/Expenses 32
    Accounting/Bookkeeping 33
    Stocking up Your vehicle 33
    Pricing Your Services 36
    Handling Fees 43
    Price Increases 44
    Missed Appointments/Cancellations 45
    Defining Your Route 45
    Using a GPS 46
    Advertising 46
    Telephones 48
    Invoices 49

    Business Cards 50
    Client Cards 51
    Payments 52
    Plugging in at Home 52
    Filling up Water at Home 52

CHAPTER FIVE
Professionalism 55

CHAPTER SIX
Capitalizing on Your Clientele 57
    Add-on Services and Products 57
    Gift Certificates 58

CHAPTER SEVEN
Scheduling and Routing 61
    Scheduling 62
    Routing 66
    Holidays 67
    Vacations 68
    Winter Appointments 68
    Appointment Books and Appointment Software 69
    Reminder Cards vs. Reminder Calls 69
    E-mail and Text Messaging 70
    Release Forms 70

CHAPTER EIGHT
Your First Day on the Road 75
    Filling Up 75
    Upon Arrival 75
    Detecting Problems During Grooming 77
    When You Are Finished 77
    Taking Care of Yourself 78
    Parking 79
    Grooming Multiple Pets 79
    Fleas 81
    Skunk Odor 81
    At the End of the Day 81

CHAPTER NINE
Managing Your Clientele...83
    Loyalty..83
    When a Pet Passes Away..83
    Newsletters...84
    Holiday Gifts..84
    Maintaining Your Client Base..85
    Fine-tuning Your Clientele..86

CHAPTER TEN
Grooming Cats in a Mobile Unit...89
    Marketing and Soliciting New Cat Clients............................90
    Pricing..93
    Extra Fees...94
    Collecting and Transporting the Cat....................................95
    Assessing Temperament and Condition................................96
    Products, Tools and Equipment..96
    Rebooking and Frequency of Grooms..................................98
    Sedation...98
    Training and Certification...98
    About Danelle German..99

CHAPTER ELEVEN
Managing Your Mobile Vehicle...101
    Mobile Grooming Tips...101
    Mobile Vehicle Tips...105
    Climate Control...107
    Driving a Trailer..108

CHAPTER TWELVE
In and Out with Style...115
    Finding the Right Trim and Schedule.................................116
    Equipment..121
    Pre-Work..124
    De-matting Techniques...124
    De-shedding Techniques...126

CHAPTER THIRTEEN
Expanding Your Business 129
    Adding Another Vehicle 129
    Hiring a Groomer 129
    Hiring an Assistant 130

CHAPTER FOURTEEN
Continuing Education 133
    Trade Shows 133
    Instructional DVDs 133
    Certification Organizations 135

A Few Words From Fellow Mobile Groomers 137
Certification Organizations 145
Trade Shows 147
Recommended Products, Manufacturers and Suppliers 151

CHAPTER ONE

Business Plan

When starting a new business it is always a good idea to put your goals down on paper. It is beneficial to have a business plan in the event you will be looking for financing for your vehicle. A business plan will also help you to reach the goals that you have set for the business. If you are starting a brand new business, chances are you will be required to submit a business plan to your lender when seeking out financing. However, if you have an established business and an established relationship with your bank and/or credit union, you may not need to submit a business plan.

Describe the business and the potential growth that it has within the first year of business and what you expect your growth is going to be within five years from now.

Prepare a market analysis in the area where you are interested in running your business. How many mobile groomers are in your area? How many grooming shops? What are the average grooming prices that the mobile groomers are charging?

Include expected start-up expenses as well as expected monthly expenses. Document projected grooming fees, the number of dogs you anticipate grooming per day, daily sales, weekly sales, monthly sales and projected annual sales.

Include projected operating expenses on a monthly basis and deduct that from your projected monthly sales. This will give you your personal income.

This is just a start to get your business plan in place. A financial advisor and/or lender may be able to further assist you in putting together a comprehensive plan for a new business.

CHAPTER TWO

Making the Right Decision

Mobile grooming is a fabulous business and can be extremely rewarding, especially when the dogs absolutely adore you. Clients say that they can't even mention my name or the dog will sit by the door all day waiting for me! It is so rewarding when the dogs are so excited to get into the van. The owners just sit in amazement. That is when you know you are doing something right!

However, there are several things that you should take into consideration before deciding if this business is for you.

When working in a grooming shop, there are normally multiple groomers and bathers working together. If a groomer is having difficulty trimming nails or plucking ears, for instance, there is always another person there who can stop what she or he is doing and help hold the dog to get the job done quickly and safely. The majority of mobile groomers work alone. If you ever come across a situation where you need help, there is no one there to help you. However, there are several companies that manufacture equipment, like the Groomers Helper®, to help you control an uncooperative dog if needed.

Will you enjoy working alone? Many groomers love to work alone and many others love to work with other people. Where do you fit in?

Mobile groomers are driving in all weather conditions—rain, sleet, snow, hail and even thunderstorms. Are you a good driver in different weather conditions?

Would you enjoy working in a small space? I love having everything within arm's reach; however, some people prefer a larger environment.

These are important things to consider. The rest will come easily. I'm sure that if you are about to read this book, you have a good feeling about mobile grooming and are trying to educate yourself so that you will be successful. I have been a mobile groomer since 1998 and love every minute of it.

CHAPTER THREE

Conversion Vehicles

Choosing a Vehicle

Finding the right vehicle is not only a personal preference but will also greatly depend upon your budget. Many different styles of vehicles are available. There are conversion companies that build trailers, vans, sprinters, box trucks and Elite vehicles. Some people require more work space than others, so you should take space into consideration when deciding upon a vehicle.

Wag'n Tails Sprinter

Sometimes situations arise when groomers must sell their vans after a short period of time due to unforeseen circumstances. These are the vans that hit the market with very low mileage and low hours on the generator. It is a great opportunity to grab a practically new van at a lower price. Two reputable websites that cater to buying and selling pre-owned grooming vans are petgroomer.com and usedgroomingvans.com.

When buying a pre-owned vehicle, make sure that the generator is in good working order and the truck/van and generator have been well maintained. Ask for maintenance records and/or the mechanic who has maintained the vehicle for the seller. It is a good idea to have a mechanic look over the vehicle to make sure there are no hidden problems that need repair.

Check with the conversion companies to see if they have trade-ins available. Many times they will offer financing on pre-owned vehicles.

Trailers are another option that would allow you to get started on a low budget. They are a bit less expensive than the vans. Trailers are very spacious and have ample storage; however, they must be towed with another vehicle that has adequate towing capacity. After 14 years of mobile grooming, I have now become so busy travelling with speaking and judging assignments, my DVD series and my grooming apparel line that I have had to cut back my grooming schedule. I decided to go with a trailer because of the lower overhead. I absolutely love the organization and the storage and am enjoying driving my own vehicle every day. At first I was not comfortable backing into driveways, so I would pull up in front of the client's house. I now have it down to a science and I can back into most driveways without a problem. I am having a lot of fun with it, so don't rule out a trailer. If I can do it, so can you!! See Chapter 11 "Managing Your Mobile Vehicle" for trailer driving tips.

Wag'n Tails Trailer

The Wag'n Tails Elite is one of the larger models available. It is equipped with a refrigerator, a microwave and even a bathroom. The grooming table is in the center of the floor, which allows a groomer to walk around the dog; this is a great feature. This model has an abundant amount of space inside as well as storage.

Wag'n Tails Elite

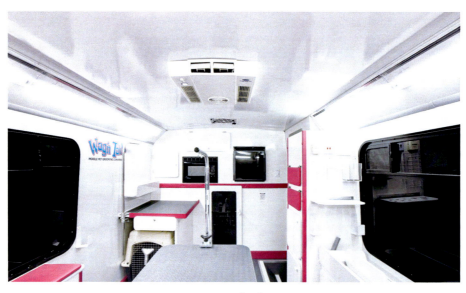

Wag'n Tails Elite

It is very exciting to purchase a new vehicle. Some manufacturers allow you to choose your favorite accent color, options and equipment. I have owned three new Wag'n Tails Pet Pro vehicles over the years mainly due to the fact that they always came out with new features that I really wanted! Selling my vehicle was never a problem. After paying off my loan I always had plenty of equity, which allowed me to easily step into my next new vehicle. That is the nice thing about mobile grooming conversions; they hold their resale value well.

Wag'n Tails Pet Pro Van

Wag'n Tails Pet Pro Van

Motor homes can easily be converted into grooming vans. My good friend, Judy Hudson, worked many years in a motor home in Tennessee. We had so much fun at grooming competitions because Judy would always have her motor home and would stay there instead of the hotel. She had her own set-up to get her dogs ready for the competitions without leaving her "hotel room." I would meet her there for coffee every morning before we had to be in the competition ring! When Judy had her daughter, Annie Kate, she brought her to work with her every day as an infant in the motor home! Judy never had to worry about leaving her with a babysitter. Motor homes are already set up for you. Judy took out her dinette to make room for her grooming table, raised her bathtub higher, put in a larger generator and a larger fresh water tank and she was good to go.

Judy Routley, another proud motor home owner

Building a conversion is another option. When building a vehicle, it is important to allow for ample storage and to have a floor plan where everything is easily accessible and within arm's reach. Be sure that the power supply is sufficient to run all the equipment that is necessary, including air conditioning. It is important to plan for plenty of outlets to plug in clippers, chargers, grooming table and dryers.

There are many options, so take the time to make the right decision based upon your budget. Keep in mind that purchasing a new truck most likely will require a loan to pay off; however, it is for a short period of time and then you own the vehicle outright just like a new car. After four or five years of having the monthly expense of a truck payment, that money will now become profit.

Generators vs. Inverters

Generators

I have had generators with all three vehicles that I have owned throughout the years. The key to owning a reliable generator is maintenance. When my generator is happy, I'm happy! I will change the oil and filters every month. Every 3 months, or 500 hours, I take my generator to be serviced at a certified service center to change the spark plugs and do a full service with filters and anything else that needs attention. Down time is very inconvenient, so maintaining the generator is critical. Most vehicles are equipped with shoreline capabilities (which allows the mobile unit to plug directly into your client's electrical power source via an extension cord), so if your generator does have a problem, plugging into someone's home is an option.

A quick tip when plugging in: try to plug in to a client's laundry room outlet where the amps are suited for a washer/dryer, which is normally 20 amps. This will prevent the possibility of tripping the circuit breaker. When plugged in, do not run the a/c and the high velocity dryer at the same time because chances are the client's breaker will trip. If the a/c does not need to be turned on, then there should not be a problem using the equipment that is needed. The a/c will draw a lot of amps. If I were to ask a client where they have a 20 amp outlet, the client most likely would not know. The laundry room is a safe place to plug in as it most likely is a 20 amp line. Always carry a 100-foot 10 gauge extension cord in the vehicle in case of emergencies when plugging in is the only option.

I try to avoid plugging in, as it can be a headache. When running the electrical cord through a client's laundry room it is impossible to close the door completely. If the client has other animals, cats or young children, this can become a problem. We sell our business as being completely self-contained, so we should try to keep it that way. Emergencies do arise and clients will understand if we have to plug in. I just try to avoid it at all costs.

Generators are a constant reliable power source. I have always had an Onan 7000 generator in my vehicles. This generator runs 58.3 amps of power. I can run my a/c, high velocity dryer and stand dryer (at the right setting) without tripping the breaker in my generator. Utilizing all this equipment at the same time keeps me extremely efficient. Generators supply all the power that you could possibly need. As mentioned, I maintain my generator on a regular schedule.

Most generators are mounted in a compartment which allows the noise to be at a minimum. In fact, I can never hear my generator running while I am in the van. Generators do best when they are used to their maximum. This means the more load you put on the generator the better. A generator should never be turned off while there is a load on it. Everything should be powered down before turning it off. It is not good for the generator to be turned off in between stops. Let it run all day; that is what it is built to do. During the summer months it is not good to turn the a/c off and on as well. The a/c owner's manual often states to wait at least 15 minutes before turning the a/c back on. The van will stay consistently cool by leaving the a/c on throughout the day. If I see that I will not be arriving at my next stop for at least 30 minutes, I will turn off the generator. There are times when I have to run an errand and, therefore, I will turn it off.

I have always had good experiences servicing my generator. My Onan repairman would take me right in if I ever had a problem and try to get me back on the road as soon as possible. I always worked four days a week so I could have my fifth day to use for emergencies. Working seven days a week will leave no room for error. (See the "Scheduling and Routing" chapter.) If you have no available days off, it is hard to reschedule appointments in case of an emergency or weather conditions.

A generator can last anywhere from 4000 to 6000 hours or more depending on how well it is maintained. I have seen a generator with almost 8000 hours on it.

Keep a detailed generator log in the vehicle. Note how many hours the generator had when it was purchased. You should log oil changes, filters and full services into the book noting the date and hours on the generator at the time of service. This is very important in order to keep the generator well maintained and also to keep records for resale purposes.

Inverters

I have never personally used a vehicle with an inverter; however, I can share facts that I have gathered from other groomers as well as from inverter experts.

Inverters are battery systems that must be charged on a daily basis (depending on how many dogs you are grooming per day and how many amps you are using throughout the day). Inverters change DC electricity, which is stored in the battery, to AC electricity, which comes from your outlets in the wall. The amount of battery banks carried will determine the longevity of your charge. The size of the inverter system will determine how many amps you can use. The larger the inverter system, the more amps you can use.

Some grooming van manufacturers build their vans strictly with inverters. Others use generators and inverters together. Some inverter systems are set up so they are charging off of your truck engine throughout the day. This means that you must let your vehicle idle while you are working so your batteries will constantly stay charged. The benefit of this is that you most likely will not run out of power during the day. However, this can cause unnecessary wear and tear on your truck and in some cases can void the warranty on your vehicle if a problem arises.

As of this date, 31 states that I am aware of have enacted laws prohibiting engine idling, so be sure to check with your state before deciding to use an inverter system. Visit www.atri-online.org to see what the laws are in your state for engine idling.

For more information on inverters visit www.xantrex.com. Xantrex are the experts on inverters.

High velocity dryers, vacuums and air conditioners draw a lot of amps. If you are running a vehicle that does not require you to idle the truck engine, your battery charge will diminish as the day goes on. It may be difficult to run an inverter system in the warmer climates where air conditioning is a necessity most of the year. Your a/c will draw from your battery all day, which may cause you to lose power during the middle of the day. Most vehicles that run solely off of inverter systems use equipment that is feasible for that particular inverter system. For example, if you see a vehicle that runs off a generator, you most likely will see a 17 amp high velocity dryer in that vehicle. If you see a vehicle that runs off an inverter system, you will see a high velocity dryer that runs off of 10 to 12 amps. When you use equipment that has lower amps, high velocity dryers for example, your drying time will be affected. If it takes me 10 minutes to dry a dog with a generator using a 17 amp HV dryer, it may take the user of an inverter system with a 10–12 amp dryer 25 minutes to dry the same dog. Over the course of a day this will cut into your profit margin.

Adding a small generator to run your a/c may be something to consider. You also might choose a vehicle that uses an inverter and generator together.

Inverter systems are low maintenance compared to generators; however, the batteries do need to be replaced over time depending on how many dogs you are grooming per day. The more dogs being groomed the more power is being used. You can only recharge batteries for so long before they need to be replaced, which can be anywhere from 2 to 3 years. Experts have said that it is best to replace all the batteries at once, which can be costly.

I know many groomers who love inverters. However, inverters have their limitations as far as the type of equipment you can use due to amperage.

Propane vs. Electric

Some of the grooming van manufacturers use propane to heat hot water and run the furnace. When using propane to heat the hot water, I would fill my tank approximately every 2 to 3 months in the warmer months and approximately once a month during the winter. The main advantage of using propane is its rapid recovery time whereas electric may take a bit longer.

Propane may also be used for the furnace; however, I found that if I turned my furnace on I would go through much more propane. I chose to use a space heater instead. The majority of the time the van will stay warm due to the dryers running, so very seldom do I need the heater on during the day.

There are also hot water heaters available that you give you the option of using either propane or electric.

I currently have a 3 gallon electric water heater which allows me to bathe at least two dogs back to back without running out of hot water. If I do run out of hot water, it normally will take about 5 minutes or so to recover.

Tip to Remember:

The power source that you choose for your vehicle is one of the most important decision you will make. The more power you have the more equipment you can run. Power will determine how productive you will be at each appointment.

CHAPTER FOUR

Getting Started

Vehicle Registration

Your vehicle must be registered as commercial in most states. Some states may require a weight for commercial vehicles prior to registration. Be sure to check with your state motor vehicle department to see what is required. If your state does require a weight, you must find a weigh station. Your motor vehicle department will be able to help you locate a weigh station.

Insurance

Vehicle insurance is mandatory. However, it is also a good idea to have professional liability insurance. There are several insurance agencies that cater to grooming professionals. Govenor Insurance has been one of our industry's leaders in insuring grooming businesses. They understand what we need as mobile groomers and offer complete coverage which includes loss of income due to a car accident/injury, escape of an animal, theft and protection of personal properties to name a few.

Registering a Business Name

When starting a business it is always a good idea to consult with an accountant so you can determine how to classify your business. Will the business be considered a DBA (which is "Doing Business As") or an LLC (Limited Liability Company), or some other form? An accountant will help you decide what is best for you.

Once you decide your classification, the next step is naming your business and registering the name with the appropriate local, county or state government office. You may be required to do a name search to be sure you are not using a business name that already exists. If you will be servicing more than one locality or servicing over state lines, then you must check with each relevant area to make sure you comply. Contact your state tax office to see if your state requires the collection of sales tax on grooming services. If so, you must collect sales tax from your clients on top of grooming services and pay these taxes to your state on a quarterly basis. Some cities and towns impose sales taxes as well; check with your municipality.

Zoning

It is important to know what the zoning is where you live. Apartment complexes, condominium complexes, neighborhoods that have homeowner associations, and similar entities may not allow residents to park their commercial vehicles in their parking areas. If this is the case, you have several options. You can have large magnets made for your vehicle instead of vinyl graphics. You can remove the magnets while you are home. This would not be my first choice for advertising; however, it is an option if you find yourself in this situation. Another option would be to rent space somewhere to park your vehicle. Check with a local gas station, RV lots, boat yards, campgrounds and storage facilities. This can be difficult, especially during the winter months when your grooming van requires heat to prevent freezing pipes, so make sure that electric and water are available at your rental facility. Locating a garage with a bay that is large enough to house your vehicle is another alternative.

Overhead/Expenses

Mobile grooming requires very little overhead compared to opening and running a grooming shop.

Your basic start-up expenditures may be as follows:

Registration	Supplies
Insurance	Invoices
Vehicle down payment	Business cards
Graphics	Grooming apparel
Advertising	Accounting fees
GPS	Client cards

Your typical monthly expenditures may be as follows:

Vehicle payment (if applicable)	Supplies
Insurance	Vehicle/Generator maintenance
Gas	Phone
Propane (if applicable)	

When I started each of my three businesses I was able to pay my expenses within the first month of business. However, it is always a good idea to save enough money to cover expenses for the first three months of starting the business just to be safe. Once my business was established, I was able to pay my expenses within just 4 to 5 days of work.

Accounting/Bookkeeping

Hiring an account to prepare your taxes would be beneficial to your business. Accountants know how to depreciate your vehicle properly and are always current on the newest tax benefits that are available to you.

Using a business checking account and a business credit card for your expenses will help keep your books organized. I use these for all my business expenses including gas, supplies, propane and so on. If you keep your business simple it will be easy to prepare your taxes. Cash is very hard to keep track of. I rely on my checking and credit card statements to show proof of expenses. Always keep receipts for supplies, products, equipment or anything else that you purchase for your business.

Stocking up Your Vehicle

Shopping for your supplies is the fun part! Here is a list of everything that I keep in my van. Remember, you can do this a little at a time if you can't afford to buy everything at once.

- Scissors, straights & curves
- Thinning shears
- Hemostats
- Andis blades (3 3/4, 4F, 5F, 7F, 10, 15, 30, 40)
- Snap-on comb set
- Combs
- Brushes
- Rat tail comb
- Andis Excel 5-Speed Clippers
- Cordless clippers
- Stripping knives   (fine, medium, coarse)
- Pumice stones
- Ear cleaner
- Ear powder
- Cotton balls
- Rubbing alcohol
- Degreaser
- Medicated shampoos
- Skin works
- Nail trimmer
- Quick stop
- First aid kit
- Motrin
- Vet wrap
- Bows/bandanas
- Business cards
- Invoices
- Client cards
- Calculator
- GPS
- Eye wash
- Eye protection

Peroxide	Surgical masks
Vinegar	Paper towel
Baking soda	Cleaners
Joy soap	Bleach
Sugar packets	Muzzles
Shampoos	Scissoring spray
Conditioners	Spray gels
Facial scrub	Hair spray
Moisture Magnet Towels (M.D.C. Romani)	Happy Hoodie (M.D.C. Romani)
Toothpaste	Ziploc bags
Toothbrushes	Slip leads
Tool box (screwdrivers, wrench, etc.)	Pens/pencils
Flashlight	Clipper parts
Clipper oil	Scissor oil
Volt meter	Spare bath spray nozzle
Spare 12V fuses	Lysol spray
Andis 5 in 1 blade wash	Fire extinguisher
Blo Pens	Stencils

It is always wise to carry at least three of each blade size, two clippers and several brushes and combs.

Keep your supplies organized. "A place for everything, everything in its place." Plastic drawers are handy to keep supplies in; however, they tend to open while you are driving. Screen locks can be screwed into each drawer and will keep them securely closed. You can purchase these at any home improvement store. They are used to lock window screens in place.

Labeling the drawers will help you to locate supplies faster. Baskets easily hold all my products, which prevents them from spilling in the cabinets while driving. Staying organized will help you stay on schedule. Searching for products will waste valuable time.

You can make a scissor holder out of Plexiglas with holes large enough to hold several shears. This allows me to keep my everyday shears organized by the type of shears they are.

I keep products such as scissoring sprays that I use on a daily basis within arm's reach.

I keep bath supplies near my bathtub so they are readily accessible. Cotton balls are stored in a plastic container. Ear cleaner, medicated shampoos, degreaser, eye wash, peroxide and hand sanitizer are all together in one location.

Pricing Your Services

When developing a price structure for mobile grooming services, a base price must be determined. This is the amount that you will leave your driveway for, no less. It can be difficult to raise your prices if you make the mistake of under-pricing your services. You are the only one who can determine what you should charge. Perform a market analysis in your area by calling several grooming shops. Get prices on several different breeds such as Maltese, Mini Poodle, Cocker Spaniel, Irish Setter, Standard Poodle, Newfoundland and Golden Retriever. Choosing these breeds or similar breeds will give you various prices, which will allow you to quote different ranges. Take the average price that you are quoted for each of these breeds and add $25 to $30. This is your mobile fee for bringing a fully equipped mobile salon to your client's doorstep. This will be the base price for those particular breeds. You can now categorize other breeds by similarities under these base prices. This is one way to set prices. (See the examples that follow.)

I prefer to charge by the hour. However, I have three hourly rates. I do not groom giant breeds; if I did, I would have four rates. If you groom cats, you will have an additional hourly rate (see the chapter on "Grooming Cats in a Mobile Unit"). My first rate is for small breeds that can be groomed in under one hour. My second hourly rate is for medium-size breeds and my third rate is for large breeds. I do not tell my clients that I charge hourly because I found in the past that they would sit and watch the clock while I was grooming their dog. However, there is one exception to this which would be discussing hourly rates for the larger breeds. This is discussed below.

I know approximately how long it normally takes me to groom every breed. Example; If the shops are averaging $50 to groom a Cocker Spaniel and I know I can groom a Cocker in one hour or so, I will set my hourly rate at $75 for that breed. This would be based on the $50 shop price plus the $25 mobile fee. I will give the client a $10 range depending upon the condition of the dog's coat. My quote would be $75 to $85 for a Cocker Spaniel. If it is a dog that has a double coat, I will give the client a $20 range with the same condition. The reason for this range is because the double coated breeds are notorious for not being groomed on a regular schedule which can be difficult to give an accurate quote. To figure out how much you are charging per minute once you go over your hourly rate, you would just take your hourly rate and divide it by 60 (60 minutes). This will give you your price per minute.

You always want to ask the client when the dog was groomed last before you even begin to quote a price. If the customer does not remember when the dog was groomed last, chances are the dog will not be in good condition. Don't be afraid to give only a starting price without a range if it is that questionable. Explain to the client that it is difficult to quote a price until you see the dog. This is for first-time clients. Once the dogs get on regular grooming schedules the price should be approximately the same at every visit. If you feel that the shops in your area are not charging enough and you know that your grooming skills are exceptionally good, then don't be afraid to increase your price to what you see fit. You do not have to base your business on what the other shops are charging, however, it is just a good guideline to setting your pricing structure.

When I started my first mobile grooming business someone suggested I quote customers the grooming price and the mobile fee for coming to their house separately. I found that it really didn't go over well. When I explained that the grooming price would be $45 and the mobile fee would be $25, they realized that this service is costing them $25 more than if they went to a shop. However, if I said the price will be approximately $70 to $80 depending upon the condition of the dog's coat, they seemed to be fine with that. This is based on my experience. If the customer questions the price, I would explain how this service differs from a grooming shop. Explain the convenience of the service, the fact that this is one-on-one grooming, there is no crate drying and the best part is that the grooming is completed within one hour or so, plus any other factors you choose to mention. It is very important to tell clients right away the benefits this service offers and how it differs from a grooming shop.

Pricing Examples

Small breeds normally take me under one hour to groom. That would include Shih Tzus, Maltese, Yorkies, Chihuahuas, and so on. If my base price is $70, that would be for dogs that take me up to one hour. For example, if it takes me 45 minutes to groom a Yorkie, I would still charge $70.

Medium-size breeds normally take me one hour to one hour and 10 minutes to groom. That would include Cocker Spaniels, Miniature Schnauzers, Westies, Lhasas, Shelties, Springer Spaniels, Cockapoos, Miniature and Toy Poodles, and so on. This hourly rate is $75.

Large breeds can take anywhere up to two hours depending on the breed. That would include Golden Retrievers, Standard Poodles, Portuguese Water Dogs, Rottweilers, Dobermans, Labs, and so on. This hourly rate is $90.

> When grooming Standard Poodles, Portuguese Water Dogs and similar breeds that may take up to two hours or more, I will tell the client I charge hourly, I will give them my hourly rate and I will tell them it will take me a minimum of two hours. The reason for this is that I want people to know up front how long it will take me so I don't hit them with a big bill at the end of the grooming appointment. At this point they can decide if this service is what they are looking for. The bottom line is if you don't charge hourly for these breeds you will lose money, no question.

Giant breeds, if you decide to do them, should be at least $15 to $20 higher than the large breeds.

Giant breeds would include Old English Sheepdogs, Bouviers, Great Pyrenees, Newfoundlands, and so on. I would also tell the client the hourly rate for the same reason as the Standard Poodle. These are breeds that I want to make sure I get paid for based on the time that I spend grooming them. They can be very time-consuming and if I don't tell clients an hourly rate, I will lose money. Just keep in mind that you can groom two to three small dogs in the same amount of time you can groom a Standard Poodle or an Old English Sheepdog.

Notice how I categorized breeds under different hourly rates based on the size of the dog and/or the amount of work that is involved. Once you determine your hourly rates you will then have to determine in which category the different breeds should fall.

These are just examples. Check to see what the pricing is in your area and be competitive. New groomers may not be as efficient as a more seasoned groomer. It may only take me one hour to groom a Cocker Spaniel where for a new groomer it may take two hours. In this case pricing by the breed may be a better solution. It takes time to build your skills and speed; you can put hourly rates into place at a later date. This may cut into your profit margin but do not be discouraged, as speed will come with experience. Never sacrifice the quality of work that you do. Quality should always come before quantity.

When making the transition from shop grooming to mobile grooming most groomers try to keep their customers from their shop. It is very important to increase their price to the new mobile grooming rates. I see this problem time and time again. When we have good customers that have been with us for years and want to continue to use our services we feel bad about increasing their price $25. The best advice I can give is to let these customers go if they don't want to pay. A new clientele is waiting, one that is looking for a mobile groomer. I know it is hard; however, if your shop customers want to continue to be a part of your clientele they will pay the additional fee. Starting your mobile grooming prices at your shop price will not benefit you as a mobile groomer. As business builds with new clients paying the new mobile price you will regret not increasing the fee for the people who are still paying the shop price. It is bad business to charge some people and not others.

Many customers who have three or four dogs are often looking for a discount. I have three kids that I took to the pediatrician without a discount. I had seven dogs at one point in my life, and my veterinarian never gave me a discount either. I never expected a discount, as I felt it was my choice and my responsibility. Giving discounts for multiple pets in one house will be no different from charging a grooming shop price rather than a mobile grooming price. We are here to benefit from the multiple pet households, not to lose money. If I have a client who has another pet that only requires a nail trim, I will absolutely do that for a nail trim charge. I have even clipped rabbit nails for clients.

Puppies are cute and fun and we all just love them. However, they are not always fun to groom. It is our job as professional groomers to make sure these puppies have a positive grooming experience. I always allow myself ample time to spend with puppies. They require table training and extra time for procedures such as drying. This is why I do not give puppy discounts. Puppies can be more work than an adult dog. If you find that the puppy you are working with was very easy and you were in and out in no time, then feel free to adjust your price. However, I have found in the past that some puppies will do really well the first time and then the next visit they are on to us and are not so good!

Bargain hunters are shopping around for the cheapest price in town and I have found them to be my least desirable customer. I am confident that my grooming skills and customer service are exceptional and my pricing reflects that. Target the people who want to pay, not the people who are looking for a deal. I don't play "let's make a deal" and you shouldn't either. Suppose someone said to me, "Wow, your price is much higher than the other mobile groomer. I only pay $50." I would reply, "That sounds like a great price. You should continue to use their service." Mobile grooming is not for everyone. A friend of mine once said, "Some people like McDonald's for dinner and some people like the Outback." We consider our service "the Outback" of grooming services!

> I had a client whose dog I had been grooming for several years. She always tipped me well and was very pleasant to work with. One day she called me from a pet store and said that she found this really cute poodle mix puppy and she wanted to take it home. I recommended that she go home and think about it. She was a stay-at-home mom and had commented in the past about how expensive it was to take her dog to the veterinarian. I reminded her of this and the fact that she would have another bill for grooming as well. She did not want to leave the store without this puppy, so of course she bought the puppy and that is when the drama began. After two weeks with the puppy she wanted to bring it back to the store because it was summertime and she wanted to be able to go away with her family and not worry about a puppy. I couldn't help but remind her of our conversation while she was in the store. She did decide to keep the puppy and when I went to groom the two dogs together she was uptight about her bill. I never received another tip from her from that point on. She kept cancelling their appointments to stretch them out from the regular four week schedule that the other dog had been on for years to now eight weeks. Her bill was more expensive now because the Cocker was becoming matted. I received a text message from her one day asking if I could groom both dogs for $50 each. I called her and explained to her that this is a business and I cannot give her a discount; it would not be fair to me or my other clients. I told her that she could get both dogs groomed at a grooming shop, which would save her money. She wanted me to do the dogs and refused to go to a shop. Each time I would book her an appointment she would cancel and stretch the dogs out a couple of more weeks. I finally told her that I could no longer groom the dogs, as they did not fit into my schedule.

When talking to people for the first time on the phone, it is important to sell yourself and sell your business. Tell potential clients, "This service is a self-contained grooming salon. I have my own electric and water supply and I am the only one who is handling your dog. This service is crate free and the dogs are all hand dried. There are no distractions or exposure to other animals. The dogs do very well in the mobile van, as they know they are home. I give them individualized attention. It normally takes me about an hour or so depending on the breed." Many people have never seen a mobile van or understand the procedure. This is why you really want to sell the service to them. If they talk about what they have been paying in the grooming shop, I always respond by saying, "Mobile grooming is a different service and does not compare to a grooming shop or their prices. I am bringing a full service salon to your home."

When you state that "there are no distractions or exposure to other animals," this means that you should not bring your dog to work with you every day. Many people seek out mobile groomers because their dogs are dog aggressive or they may even have an auto immune issue where they cannot be around other animals. The only time I have brought one of my dogs to work with me is when I had a vet appointment for that day. I could run to the vet in between appointments, or I have even dropped my dog off for a couple of hours while I was working. I always looked at my schedule to make sure that the dogs I had on my book for that day would not be distracted and/or disturbed by having another animal in the van.

Be aware of your "neighbors." They are always trying to strike a deal because after all "I am right next door." This is your business and stick to your guns! Keep your price structure consistent with every dog you groom.

I do not charge extra for de-shedding and carding services, as I believe that these techniques should be part of the grooming process for the breeds that require this. This technique gets incorporated into my price structure. I have a client with a Golden Retriever that is on a 5-week schedule. She asked if I could "just bathe him" instead of a full groom. I agreed to this without realizing what the consequences were going to be. Not only did I have hair all over my van but I had hair all over me. It was not the proper way to groom this breed, and I felt that I really did not do the dog any justice by not de-shedding it properly. We always learn from our mistakes.

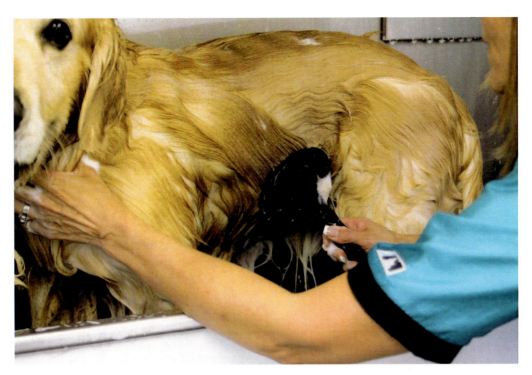
De-Shedding Techniques

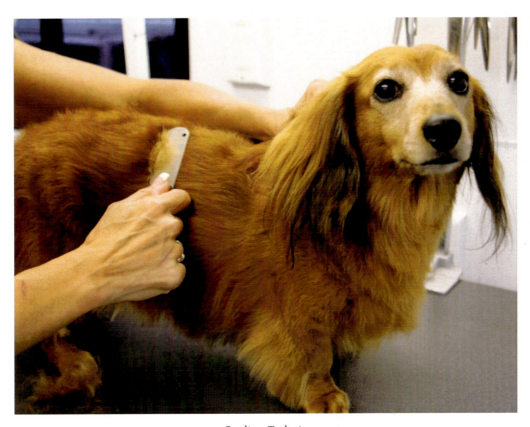
Carding Techniques

How much does it cost to run this business on a monthly basis? How much money do I want to get paid per week? If my monthly expenses are $2000 and I would like to make $1000 per week, I would need to bring in $6000 per month. Let's look at some scenarios.

If I charge $60 per dog (base price)
Groom 6 dogs per day = $360 per day
$360 x 4 days per week = $1,440 per week
$1,440 per week x 4 weeks = $5,760 per month
$5,760 x 12 months = $69,120
Your annual net sales = $69,120

$5,760 per month – $2,000 (average expenses) = $3,760 profit per month
$3,760 divided by 16 days per month (4 days a week) = $235 per day profit
$3,760 x 12 months = $45,120 gross per year!

The $60 stated above is an example of a base price, which means this is the price that I will leave my driveway for, no less. This is based on a four day work week grooming six dogs a day with an estimate of $2,000 monthly expenses. The expenses may be lower or a bit higher; this is just an example.

If I charge $70 per dog (base price)
Groom 6 dogs per day = $420 per day
$420 x 5 days per week = $2100 per week
$2,100 per week x 4 weeks = $8,400 per month
$8,400 x 12 months = $100,800
Your annual net sales = $100,800

$8,400 per month – $2,000 (average expenses) = $6,400 profit per month
$6,400 divided by 20 days per month (5 days a week) = $320 per day profit
$6,400 x 12 months = $76,800 gross per year!

The $70 stated above is another example of a base price. This scenario is based on a five day work week grooming six dogs a day with an estimate of $2000 monthly expenses. The expenses may be lower or a bit higher; this is just an average.

Keep in mind that most dogs will average $10 to $30 higher than the base price, which could increase your daily income substantially. As the business starts to build, grooming seven to eight dogs a day would be the average of what of most groomers would do. I enjoy grooming six to seven dogs per day; however, the number of dogs groomed per day is a personal preference.

How many days per week are you willing to work? Only you can answer this question. Working Saturdays will also be a matter of personal preference. I was never forced to work Saturdays unless I was making up a day due to weather. Because so many people work from home or are stay-at-home moms/dads, having to work on Saturday was never an issue for me. I have also had clients who have housekeepers and nannies who are home during the day to give me the dog. If you do run into a situation where people who work Monday through Friday want to use your service, you could try my solution: I have had them meet me during their lunch break. If they must leave before I am done, I will put the dog in the house and lock up. Working one or two Saturdays per month is always an option. This is your business and you can decide what days work best for you.

Handling Fees

If you have dogs that are difficult, you may want to charge a handling fee. Some examples of difficult dogs are:

>Old dogs with hip dysplasia
>Aggressive dogs that need to be muzzled
>Dogs that just don't like the grooming process and will not sit still

My rule of thumb: If I feel stressed and/or my back hurts when I am done from struggling with an animal, I will charge a handling fee. I may even decide not to book them another appointment depending on how bad the experience was. Remember to be selective as to what dogs you keep (see the chapter on "Managing Your Clientele"). It is not necessary to keep every dog that you groom. This is why it is important to ask the client over the phone if the dog has behavior problems. If someone tells you over the phone that their dog does not do well with grooming and that no one will groom the pet, you need to discuss handling fees. Many people with difficult dogs will seek out mobile groomers, as they feel their pets will do better when not in a shop environment with other dogs. These difficult dogs most likely will do better over a period of time; however, you need to charge for the extra effort. I have rehabilitated many dogs over the years, including the dogs that no one wanted to groom and even the dogs that had had to be sedated their entire life. I weaned them off of sedation and they now do fine.

Working alone can be challenging at times, especially when working with difficult pets. If a dog is too much to handle, don't be afraid to tell the owner.

With difficult dogs, or any dogs for that matter, it is all about consistency and trust. When you are consistent with the dogs they will start to know what is expected of them. Once they get accustomed to the routine of you coming to their home they start to realize "hey, this isn't so bad." They will do better and better at each visit. Be patient and work with them; however, if you still feel that you do not think you can handle a dog properly, you should discuss your concern with the client and refer him or her elsewhere.

> When I was a new groomer I had a Shih Tzu that was just terrible. She was my chiropractor's dog. I had to use a cat muzzle on her because she had a very short muzzle. She would scream and try to bite me every second. I was constantly jumping with that awful startling feeling that you get in your stomach. I could barely get her head groomed without her trying to bite me. I was even afraid of her with a muzzle on. Every time I left this appointment, I was almost in tears. She was so bad she even would bite the owners. I groomed her about six times. At the end of the last visit I brought the dog up to the door and said, "I'm really sorry but I can't groom her any more. She is either going to hurt herself or hurt me. I think it is best for you to take her to a vet who has a groomer on staff so she can be sedated." They looked at me and apologized over and over again.

Mobile grooming is not for every dog. Some owners think that it is better for their older dog with hip dysplasia to have a mobile groomer come to the house. However, I have found that these dogs do better in a shop environment. In a grooming shop the dogs are waiting between the steps of getting prepped, bathed, dried and groomed. They are given a lot of time during the day to rest in between each step of the process. With mobile grooming the dogs are groomed from start to finish without much time to sit. When dogs suffer from arthritis and hip issues this can be very hard on them, especially the larger breeds. Use your best judgment on these breeds and do what is best for them. If you feel that they will do better in a grooming shop, then discuss your concerns with the owner.

Price Increases

You should increase your prices on an annual basis. If you make this your practice, people will expect it. If you increase your prices annually, a 5% increase is customary. If you have not increased your prices in two to three years, you may want to consider raising them $5 to $10 across the board.

Every business has price increases. Our cost of living expenses consistently increase whether for groceries, insurance, gas, even our hair salons. The difference between these businesses and groomers is that they don't tell us that their price has increased. They just increase their prices and we pay it. We, as groomers, feel that we need to send price increase notices out as a courtesy.

I'm not really sure why that is but that seems to be the case. I will stick a price increase label on their reminder card or put it on their invoice for their next visit. I do this because after you have had clients for a long time, their price always seems to be the same. The dogs are on great schedules with minimal matting. Many people will leave me a check if they are not home, and they automatically make the check out to the usual amount. I give them notice so they know for the next visit what their new price will be.

Missed Appointments/Cancellations

If a client is not home when I arrive for the appointment, I will wait up to 15 minutes. I will not wait longer than 15 minutes because that would affect the rest of my day. I will leave a message on the client's phone stating the time that I was there and that this person should call to reschedule. If I have the client's cell phone I will call to see if she or he is on the way home. Missed appointment fees are something that every individual will have to decide whether they want to charge or not. If someone misses three appointments, I will not reschedule them. I have not had to charge for missed appointments in the past. However, you can charge 50% of the groom price for missed appointments that must be paid before the next appointment. In the case of good loyal clients who have been with you for a while, you may not wish to charge them. This is considered a professional courtesy. However, if it becomes a problem, with more than three missed appointments, then you must make a decision whether to charge a fee.

When starting a business it is a good idea to have policies in place. State the policies up front so clients are fully aware of them. Missed appointments and cancellation information should be stated in your policy. I prefer to have 24 hours notice for a cancellation so I can re-route myself. However, there are times when this is not possible. One example would be weather conditions. If a dog is deathly afraid of thunderstorms, the client will call me when the storm comes through worried about how the dog will act. In that situation there is not a lot either of us can do about it. There are times that I can move that appointment to the end of the day once the storm passes through. It can make a mess out of your day, but sometimes situations arise that are out of our control.

Defining Your Route

Before speaking to your first client you must define your route. This is the most vital step to starting your business. Remember that we do not get paid for driving. The farther we drive the less money we will make. A ten to fifteen mile radius would be ideal; however, depending upon where you live, it may be more or less. If you live in the suburbs it is much easier to define a smaller area. When I moved from Dallas my van had 24,000 miles on it after four years of grooming because of the fact that I groomed in a ten mile radius.

Once you define the area that you decide to service it is important to stick to it. Pick highways as the farthest point to make it easy. When using highways as your boundaries, you can tell a client, "I service from Route 71 to Route 15." This may not work in some cases. Using towns, counties and/or zip codes as boundaries are other options. Calls will consistently come in from potential clients who live outside your route. They may even say that they are only .5 mile from your area. Once you go over your line you will get calls from that area which you really don't want to service. Keep your route tight. I have had people beg and plead for me to groom their dogs that are out of my area. If they really want to use my service I will have them meet me at a strip mall within my boundaries and I will groom their dogs in the parking lot while they shop. I have also had clients move outside my route. They wanted to continue to use my services, so I decided to charge them by the mile in addition to their grooming price. I did that a couple of times and before I knew it I had people calling me from that area. I stopped doing that right away and had these people meet me at a convenient location within my route.

I have had two clients move from New Jersey to Pennsylvania. One meets me at their daughter's house within my route, and the other one meets me at a strip mall. Where there is a will, there is a way!

When starting a new mobile grooming business it can be very tempting to take on everyone who calls. Be patient and be selective. Once you become busy you will not want to drive to areas that are out of your route, so it is best not to take those clients on from the start. It is hard to let people go after you have been grooming their dog for a while.

Using a GPS

It's always great to have a GPS system to get to appointments quickly. Even though you may think you know your area like the back of your hand, there are often short cuts from one house to another that you may not realize.

Advertising

The graphics that you choose for your vehicle will be your best form of advertising. Eye-catching graphics are the best investment in this business. Choose vibrant colors and be sure the phone number is large and clearly seen from the front, sides and rear of the vehicle. Drive the vehicle everywhere. I always drove my kids to and from school, soccer games, school events, holiday concerts at school, grocery store, bank, post office and shopping centers. Each time I would have the truck out for the day I would come home to phone calls. Leaving the vehicle at major shopping centers for a few hours also brought in many calls. Let your graphics do the work for you. I had business cards designed as magnets and stuck them all over my van. This allowed people to take them while the van was parked. This was especially helpful while I was grooming in the van. Many people would come knocking on my door while I was grooming a dog to get a business card. It would completely distract the dog that I was grooming, which would take me a bit to calm down. Not only do business card magnets prevent distractions but also potential clients will most likely go home with one and place it on their refrigerator.

Local newspapers are very interested in promoting new businesses in town, so take advantage of that. Explain the service that you offer and how convenient it is for pet owners. Stress how nice it is for their pets to be groomed in their own driveway. Really sell yourself and show your passion for your career.

I never put a paid ad in the yellow pages; however, my business was listed in the white pages with my phone number. Yellow page listings often reach many towns/zip codes which may be out of your route. This will result in unnecessary callbacks to areas that you do not service.

Visit all the veterinarians in your area and leave business cards with them. Having a good reputation with the veterinarians in town is something that every groomer should strive for. A veterinarian can make or break your business. If injuries come into their office on a regular basis, the vet will not recommend your services. If you do a nice job and the clients are happy, veterinarians will pass your name along. I always have had a great reputation with my veterinarians and was always highly recommended.

If a veterinarian has a groomer on staff, you should still leave your business cards with them. Many dogs require mobile grooming. Some dogs get car sick or have auto immune problems and can't be around other animals. There are the older dogs, the elderly people who don't drive, dogs that have separation anxiety, and so on. There is always a need for mobile groomers. Many people just don't want to leave their pets in a shop all day.

Contact the pet sitters in your area. They are a great team to network with. People who hire pet sitters to walk their dogs while they are at work are potential clients. These pet owners are looking for the best services available for their pets. I have had pet sitters knocking on my door while I am grooming asking if I am taking on new customers. I have noticed that many of my clients have a check for me and a check for the pet sitter sitting on their kitchen counters.

Local radio stations are another form of advertising and are always happy to promote new businesses. Ask if they will do a live broadcast for your business. They will often repeat the broadcast at a later date.

Websites are a way for people to tune into your service, see your van, check out what you offer and get that warm feeling when they see you and pictures of the pets that you groom. Designing a website is something that many people can do; however, it is important that the website designer whom you hire also knows how to get you into the search engines. Many people can design websites, but not everyone has the knowledge to get you into the search engines. Show pictures of your grooms so people will be able to see the quality of your work. You can even have a short video clip of yourself giving an overview of your business.

Start a Facebook page. This is another way for your clients to see what you are doing and to send you messages and pictures of their dogs.

I never spent a lot of money on advertising, as my van was my moving billboard. I removed my phone number from two of my vans because I couldn't keep up with the calls. I started a waiting list several times. I found that I never looked at the list, so I stopped promising people that I would call them if an opening became available. This is a good problem to have and a popular problem with most mobile groomers.

Telephones

I prefer to have a land line for my business in my home. The land line is strictly a basic line with no added features, with the exception of voice mail. This has kept my expenses down. I don't answer the phone; however, I have a detailed message on my voice mail so I can screen my calls. I do this so I can prepare myself as to what to say to the client when I call back. My message sounds like this: "Hi, thank you for calling the Puppy Spa, a mobile pet styling service for your pampered pet. I am out grooming right now, so please leave me a message with the breed of dog that you have and the area where you live, and I will return your call at the end of the day. This service is catered to dogs that are groomed on a regular grooming schedule. Please note that I do not groom cats. If you are a current client and you need to reach me regarding your appointment for today, you may call me on my cell phone at _____. Thank you for calling the Puppy Spa, and have a great day." To eliminate calls that are outside your area, you can also add the areas that you service in your message.

The reason why I mention the fact that I do not groom cats is so I will not have to return unnecessary calls. If you only groom certain size dogs, you can say, "This service is for dogs under 50 pounds." Include as much information as you can on your voice mail to save you time.

Once I receive the messages and the potential clients tell me where they live and the type of dog they have, I can call them back and be prepared as to what to say. They may be out of my area, or they may have a breed like a Newfoundland that weighs 200 pounds that I prefer not to do. I will tell them right away, "I'm sorry, I cannot service your area or that breed," without getting into a lengthy conversation before all that information is revealed. Often when we are caught off guard by answering a phone call, we may quote a lower price than if we had given it a bit of thought first. This will also give you a chance to look up the client's area to see if this person is within your route.

I always give my cell phone number in case my customers for that day need to reach me. They may be trying to contact me to say they had to leave the house but will leave the back door open, maybe they are running late and will not be home for another 20 minutes, or something else that will affect my day if they have no way to reach me.

Using a cell phone as your business line is another option. Eliminating a land line will save you money. However, you should have a detailed message for your business calls. I would suggest not answering the phone if you don't recognize the number. Instead of saying, "I'm out grooming right now," you can say, "I'm busy grooming right now." I do not take client calls during the day as it slows me down. I return calls in the evening. It would be a good idea to put all your client numbers in your cell phone so you know if they are trying to reach you.

I always leave an away message on my phone line when I will be out of town. My message will say, "The Puppy Spa will be closed from Friday May 21st through Tuesday May 25th. I will return your call on Wednesday the 26th." I know how hectic it can be when preparing for a trip, so I try not to forget to do this. Otherwise, people will call several times wondering why I am not returning their calls.

When my client base becomes full I will put a new message on my voice mail stating, "I am not taking on new customers at this time; however, feel free to check back at a later date." Although, if you find that you can take on a new dog occasionally, depending upon the breed, you may not want to leave this message. You may get a call with a little Chihuahua that you could get done in 25 minutes. In this case you can leave a message stating, "If an appointment becomes available I will return your call." This will allow you to fill small gaps in your schedule if needed.

Invoices

Invoices can be designed by a local print shop in the area. I use half sheet (4.25" x 5.5"), carbonless two-part invoices. I have all the information necessary as well as a box for the client's next scheduled grooming appointment. On this invoice I have categories that I will check off if I am adding on additional fees. I also have an "Other" box for retail or whatever I did that was not a category on the invoice. I give the top white copy to the client and keep the yellow bottom copy for my records. This is one way to show the clients what I offer. I will also use the invoice as a way to announce a price increase in effect at their next grooming. It looks very professional and people like having a receipt.

```
                    ┌─────────────────────────────────────────────┐
                    │  The                                         │
                    │   PUPPY              _____ Date        │
                    │    Spa               _____             │
                    │                      _____             │
                    │ "Mobile Pet Styling For Your Pampered Pet"   │
                    │   Address            _____             │
                    │   City, State, Zip   _____             │
                    │                      Pet Name/Breed          │
                    │                                              │
                    │   Full Service Grooming _____       │
                    │    ❏ Advantix Application                    │
                    │    ❏ Flea Treatment                          │
                    │    ❏ Brushing/Detangling                     │
                    │    ❏ Pre-Cut/Brush                           │
                    │    ❏ Carding/Stripping                       │
                    │    ❏ Teeth Brushing                          │
                    │    ❏ Medicinal Soak                          │
                    │    ❏ Scissoring                              │
                    │    ❏ Handling/Behavior                       │
                    │    ❏ Other _____          │
                    │        _____          │
                    │   ┌──────────────────┐  Sub Total _____    │
                    │   │ Your next        │                       │
                    │   │ appointment      │  Sales Tax _____    │
                    │   │ is scheduled for │                       │
                    │   │ _____  │  Total _____    │
                    │   │ at _____  │                       │
                    │   └──────────────────┘                       │
                    │              Thank You,                      │
                    │             Jodi Murphy                      │
                    │          MASTER PET STYLIST                  │
                    │              Phone #                         │
                    └─────────────────────────────────────────────┘
```

Business Cards

When designing business cards always include your business logo and/or name, phone number, website, qualifications, mailing address and e-mail address. It is always nice to include a catch phrase, such as "Mobile Pet Styling for Your Pampered Pet." On the back of my card I list the services that I offer. I do not have a place for the client's next appointment because I have that on my invoice. I use business cards to hand out to potential clients who approach me when they see me out and about and also to leave at places like the veterinarians' offices.

Client Cards

Client cards are large index cards which allow you to record all necessary client information, pet health records, specific grooming instructions as well as driving directions for each appointment. These cards are available through Barkleigh Productions.

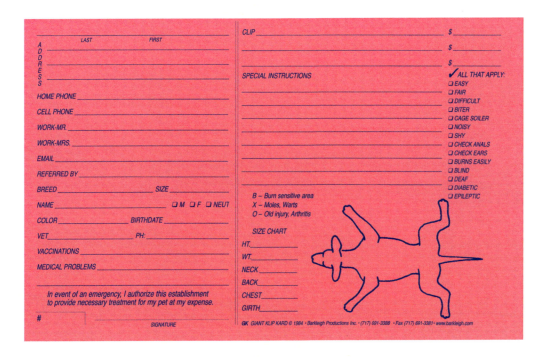

Payments

When I first opened my business I decided to accept credit cards. I had very few credit card sales during my first year in business, so I decided not to renew my contract and only accept checks or cash. Unless you sell retail items, I think most people are very comfortable paying by check. Technology has changed so much since I started my first business. Many cell phones have the ability to accept credit cards by adding a simple device to your phone. The fees are minimal and it is very convenient. Check with your cell phone company to see if this is an option for you.

I have had very few returned checks. My bank offers a check retrieval program in which they will recoup the funds for me if I have received a bounced check. Many of my clients have been with me for many years, so if a problem come up, I know where they live! I do add a $25 returned check fee if necessary. If you feel more comfortable asking for driver's license information from a first-time client, then feel free to do that. If a client bounces a check three times, I will not reschedule that person. I can only remember two clients whom I had to let go because this was becoming a problem.

Plugging in at Home

Using your shore line at home to plug in during the winter months or even to groom your own dogs is a nice feature and will save hours on your generator. However, just like plugging into a client's house, you can only utilize so many amps before you trip the breaker. Several of my own dogs need to be groomed on a regular schedule. I hired an electrician to install a dedicated line solely for my grooming van. I can now groom my own dogs at home without running my generator, which saves me many hours as well as unnecessary wear and tear on my generator. A dedicated line is not necessary if you are just plugging in at home to run your space heaters.

Filling up Water at Home

Installing a hot/cold spigot in my garage enabled me to fill up my tank with warm water during the winter months. Filling up with warm water prevents my hot water heater from turning on as often. I keep my hose on a hose reel in the garage and fill up with warm water every morning. Keeping the hose in the garage prevents it from freezing in the winter. When it snows here in New Jersey, the roads are heavily salted, so you can only imagine what my van looks like at the end of the day. With a warm water hose I can spray down the van after work to keep it looking clean and professional all winter long.

Tip to Remember:

Preparation for starting your new business should be done months in advance to ensure that you have all your bases covered. All policies and procedures should be set prior to taking on your first client. Pricing your services should be well thought out. It is very hard to increase your pricing once you have set your price structure. Consulting with an accountant prior to starting your business will eliminate year-end tax problems. The information provided in this Chapter is very important and will help you start a successful business.

CHAPTER FIVE

Professionalism

As mobile groomers we should always present ourselves in a professional manner while at a client's home. First impressions are very important, so dressing professionally in nice grooming apparel is important. When I was working in Dallas, one day I went to a home that had a Toy Poodle and a Chihuahua. I took the cute little Toy Poodle from the client and walked to my van. When I returned she was all smiles and said, "I was so relieved when I saw you cuddle her up as you walked away talking so nicely to her. The last groomer who came had a cigarette in one hand, grabbed her out of my arms and held her like a football. All I wanted to do was go and take her back into the house." That really took me by surprise and I always kept that thought in the back of my mind. People care so much about their pets. They want them to be in good hands. If you show up in a T-shirt and jeans with dog hair all over you, it gives a poor impression. You could be the nicest person and the best groomer, but first impressions mean everything.

When driving commercial vehicles you always want to be a courteous driver. Your business name and phone number are all over your vehicle. Always act in a professional manner even if you have to fight off road rage.

As you develop a steady clientele you will become very friendly with people. When you are in a customer's home, you become a friend. I have customers bring me lunch, drinks, coffee, and so on. They are very considerate. It is nice to develop friendships. However, it can become awkward when you have to raise prices and deal with business issues, so it's always best to keep business business.

When you start with new clients, they will often talk about the prior groomer. It is best not to comment and stay professional. Chances are if they are talking about the prior groomer, they will talk about you. I have a group of women who are all friends. It's funny because they often talk about each others' dogs. Good and bad! I have found that the best way to handle this is to stay neutral. I just say "he's a good dog" or something else positive. Be careful and stay professional at all times.

CHAPTER SIX

Capitalizing on Your Clientele

Add-on Services and Products

The vast majority of mobile groomers have a standing clientele, which means that they have pre-booked appointments on a regular basis. I very rarely take on new customers unless they are highly recommended. I will only take them on if I can fit them into my route easily and I know they will be on a regular schedule. Mobile groomers can only take on a certain number of clients (see chapter on "Managing your Clientele"). This brings groomers to believe that their business has no growth potential and that it has capped out. There are always ways to make additional money on the clients that you have. You can provide many add-on services for your clients.

We are limited as to how many retail items we can carry; however, I like to sell certain products that I use to my clients. My clients are always asking me about shampoos and brushes. Some clients prefer to bathe their dogs in between appointments, especially Yorkies, Chihuahuas, Labs, etc. When attending trade shows I stock up on brushes, combs and eight ounce bottles of shampoos. Oftentimes show specials are available that will save you money on your retail items.

Teeth brushing is another service that I offer my clients. I purchase soft youth toothbrushes for less than one dollar at the grocery store. I store the toothbrushes in a drawer and write the pet's name on a brush with a Sharpie. I will not brush a dog's teeth that have very bad tartar build-up and should have professional cleaning. I explain to the client that I can help prevent plaque build-up; however, I cannot remove it. Once clients have the teeth professionally cleaned, then I can try to keep the plaque down by regular brushing. I also try to encourage them to brush at home as well. On toy breeds I will use a gauze pad with some toothpaste and wipe the teeth down instead of using a big toothbrush.

When I lived in Dallas I offered Frosty Paws, which is a doggie ice cream cup, during the summer months. Clients absolutely loved it. I told them that they should let me know the night before their appointment so I could pack my cooler. I would give the dogs their Frosty Paw before they had their bath.

"Stenciling," "Tatooing," and adding a "Splash of Color" are other ways to make extra money. Blo pens are the best thing to use. However, they can be hard to find, so you can use pastels, chalk or even spray color from a beauty supply store instead to give ears a splash of color to match a bow. During the holiday seasons you can buy stencils and give the dogs tattoos!

A big seller during tick and flea season is Advantix or other products of that nature. If I am grooming a dog and find a tick, I will bring into the house the appropriate dosage for that animal when I finish grooming the dog. I will tell the clients that I found a tick (or ticks) and ask them if the dog is on a preventive. If they say no, I sell them a single application. I ask them to apply it the next day, as the bath strips the oils from the dog's skin and the oils in the skin are what spread the medication. Purchasing a complete pack of any flea/tick medication can be expensive. I find that most clients are very happy to purchase one application. It is not only affordable but will also save them a trip to the store.

Nail grinding is a great service to provide your clients. Many dogs will tolerate nail grinding better than nail clipping. Grinding the back nails is for the safety and comfort of the dog while grinding the front nails is for the safety and comfort of the owners. Nail grinding will prevent the dog from scratching and causing skin irritations, especially on freshly clippered poodle faces. Clipping nails can often leave sharp edges that will easily scratch the owners and children, so grinding the front nails will prevent this. Be careful when you are grinding nails on dogs that have a longer coat. It is very easy for the coat to get caught in the grinder, which can really hurt the dog.

Medicated shampoos, degreasers and natural flea shampoos are not included in the regular grooming price. These products are considered extra.

Gift Certificates

Gift certificates are a great service to offer your clients and especially come in handy around the holidays. It's a good idea to put an expiration date on the certificate. It is very hard to keep track of them for long periods of time. A customer once purchased a certificate for her daughter's Springer Spaniel. The dog was not a client of mine and was not maintained at all. It was a one-time grooming appointment and a lot of work which was hard to fit into my schedule. I now only offer certificates to my client dogs, which expire in six months. Many clients have friends and family who use my services. This makes a great gift for them. Gift certificates are applied to the total price of the groom. If someone buys a $200 gift certificate, you can treat it as a gift card and deduct the grooming appointments as they are being used.

Tip to Remember:

Add on services will help you bring in more income. Include your add-on services on your invoice so your clients will know what is available to them.

CHAPTER SEVEN

Scheduling and Routing

When first starting a mobile grooming business, scheduling and routing can be very difficult. It takes time to get new clients on regular schedules. Most clients may start out on a six week schedule and then realize how convenient this service is and change to a five week schedule. It will also take time to remember who lives near whom so you can make your route flow easily. Don't be discouraged if things are not flowing well in the beginning. It takes up to one year to really establish your clientele and understand your route.

There are key questions you want to ask new clients when booking an appointment.

1. Are you familiar with mobile grooming services?
2. Is your dog current on vaccinations?
3. When was your dog groomed last?
4. Do you have your dog groomed on a regular schedule?
5. How often do you have your dog groomed?
6. Does your dog have any health problems that I should know about?
7. Does your dog have any behavior problems that I should know about?
8. How old is your dog?

This gives you enough information to get started. Once clients book the appointment you can ask them more questions the day you arrive for grooming.

Scheduling

When I schedule appointments for clients I will give them a few options for the week they are looking for. I never say, "What day and time do you want me to come?" It is always best for people to see that you are busy, even if you are slow during the first few months of starting your business. If people think you have too much availability, they will be more apt to cancel appointments and expect to be rescheduled right away. When I see an establishment that is busy, such as a restaurant or hair salon, I immediately think that they must be very good. This is the same impression people get when they speak to groomers. Potential clients may not realize you are slow due to the fact that this is a new business and, instead, assume it is because you are not very good. This being said, it is best to let them think you are busy.

> I had a client ask me to take on her friend's Shih Tzu. She told me that her friend was having so many problems with groomers. I really had no availability at all and kept telling her no. One time she begged me to talk to her friend and I did. I told her friend that I would call her if things slowed down and I could get her in. Of course, I never did because things never slow down. Two years later my client begged me again to call her friend. I felt bad so I called her up and squeezed her into my schedule. As I arrived at her house, and was getting my van ready, I saw the owner outside with the little Shih Tzu on a leash. I stepped out of my van to greet her and I just could not believe what I was seeing . . . it was a really good friend from high school! We both just were in shock. I had been putting this girl off for two years. I didn't even recognize her voice when we spoke on the phone. It was so funny, we laugh about it all the time. It was such a great reunion and I really enjoy the time I get to spend with her every month. I actually try to book myself enough time on her appointment day so I can have lunch with her and visit.

Clients will often share their alarm codes, garage codes and keys in order for me to groom their dog when they are not home. This is something that will come with time. You have to gain trust with your clients before they offer you their keys. I found that once people tried the service and saw how convenient it was they offered a way to get into the house in case they were not home. I keep their alarm codes on their client cards. I keep all client cards at my house. This is very important. If you have confidential information, you do not want to keep it in your van. I only bring the cards with me for clients I am grooming for that day. Some people will leave their back doors open for me, which is another option. I find when clients are not home I am able to stay on schedule. I have run into situations where I can't find the dog when I arrive. You may want to ask the client to put the dog in a crate or gate the dog in the laundry room so this won't happen to you. I have had to go outside and ring the doorbell so the dog would come barking at the front door so I could catch it!

I prefer to give a one-hour window for arrival. If I feel I am going to be later than the hour, I will call the clients and tell them that I am running behind. Sometimes they will say, "Okay, I will leave the back door open because I have to run out." You always want to call if you are going to be late. I will also call if I feel that I will be ahead of schedule to make sure the clients will be home. I do give people my cell phone number so they can call to check how I'm running or in the event they have to leave the house. If you arrive at an appointment and you have clients tell you that they have to run out but will be home before you are finished, be sure to tell them how long you think you will be. Always tell them sooner rather than later. I have been to homes where clients left to run an errand and I had to wait almost 30 minutes before they came back. I had no way of putting the dog in the house, as they locked up before they left.

> I can laugh about this story now, although it really wasn't funny at the time. I groomed a little Poodle for the first time in a senior citizen assisted living community. The husband and wife were living in the condo. They had to be around 80 years old. When I was finished with the dog, no one was home. I waited for 20 minutes; still no one home. I was getting worried because I was falling behind schedule. I finally went to the neighbors' home and they told me that my clients' daughter came and took them out for the day. Did everyone forget about this little Poodle? Didn't the daughter wonder where their dog was? I was almost ready to just take the dog with me for the rest of the day until the neighbor offered to take the dog until the owners got home. The daughter finally called me to send me a check. She didn't apologize or think anything was wrong with that at all. Needless to say I never went back.

My clients have three appointments in my book. I know some groomers who like to book clients out for six months to a year. I am afraid that if my schedule changes I would have to reschedule all those appointments for that client. Three appointments works great for me. My clients only know of their next appointment. Pre-booking everyone three months out really helps you fine-tune your route. This will also help determine whether or not you can take on new customers, as you will be able to see your availability once all your clients are accounted for.

When I give my clients their next appointment I will make a check mark next to their names in my appointment book. This confirms that I have left them a date and time on their invoice. If I don't see a mark near their names, I know that I need to call them to make sure they know they have an appointment scheduled.

While in Ohio I serviced a doggie day care center once a week to groom dogs that were in day care. The day care operators would have their clients call me to set up their appointments. It worked out really well. I sat in the same place all day. The day care center wanted to offer their clients a perk, so they were happy that I agreed to do it. Everyone benefited from the situation.

When scheduling appointments for each day, be sure to look at the breeds that you are scheduling. Fill your day so you are not going to have more than one big job. Mixing small bath dogs with haircuts will allow your day to run smoothly. It will be a very long day if you have two Cocker Spaniels, two Poodles, and two Bichons. Try to break it up with easy dogs that don't take you very long. If you have a Standard Poodle or a Portuguese Water Dog on your book, then you may not want to book 6 dogs that day; you may only want to book 4 or 5. Otherwise, make sure the rest of your day you have easy haircuts that won't bog you down. Be easy on yourself at first until you get things down to a science.

Here are examples of typical days for me.

9:00–10:00	Cairn
	Maltese
10:00–11:00	Westie
11:00–12:00	Airedale
1:00–2:00	Cocker Spaniel
2:30–3:30	Bichon
3: 30–4:30	Maltipoo

My first appointment has two dogs. A little Maltese with very fine hair that only takes me about 30 minutes and a Cairn Terrier. Both dogs together take me about 1 hour and 15 minutes. I should arrive at my next appointment at approximately 10:15-10:30.

My second appointment is a Westie that lives about 3 miles from my first job. She takes me about 45 minutes. Westies dry very fast so they are easy to get done quickly. I anticipate arriving at my next appointment at approximately 11:30.

My third appointment is an Airedale that takes me about 1 hour and 10 minutes. He lives about 10 miles from my second appointment. I will arrive at my next appointment between 1:00-1:15.

My fourth appointment is a Cocker Spaniel that lives about 10 miles from my third appointment. He is in a traditional suburban trim and takes me 1 hour. I will have no problem arriving at my next appointment by approximately 2:30.

My fifth appointment is a Bichon that lives about 5 miles from my fourth appointment and takes me 1 hour. I should be able to arrive at my last appointment no later than 3:45.

My sixth appointment is a Maltipoo that lives about 3 miles from my fifth appointment and takes me 1 hour.

This day was taken right out of my appointment book. Believe it or not this is not a great route for me because the Airedale is a bit out of my way. If you notice, I have to travel 10 miles to get to him and 10 miles back to get to my next appointment. He was one of my first clients when I first started. I mostly worked east of my house. The Airedale lived west of me. When I moved farther east it created a bit of a problem with my schedule. I just love this dog and the owner. He is in my Airedale DVD. The owners let me take him to shows to use as a demo dog, so I don't mind going out of my way in this case.

Here is another day right out of my appointment book.

    9:00–11:00   Standard Poodle
    11:00–12:00   Bichon
                        Schnoodle
    1:00–2:00   Shelty
    2:00–3:00   2 Yorkies
    3:00–4:00   Havanese

This is a really tight route. My Standard Poodle takes me about 2 hours. I should be finished with him at approximately 11:00 and be able to arrive at my next appointment by 11:15.

My second appointment is two dogs, a Bichon in a traditional Bichon trim, 4F body with scissored legs, full head. She normally takes me 1 hour and 15 minutes. The Schnoodle is easy and takes me 45 minutes. This is the family that moved to Pennsylvania and meets me in town at a strip mall that is 1 mile from my first appointment. I should be finished with these two dogs by approximately 1:00.

My third appointment is 1 mile from my second appointment and takes me under 1 hour. I will have no problem leaving this appointment by 2:00.

My fourth appointment lives about a mile from my third appointment. They take me about 1 hour and 15 minutes. I should be able to arrive at my last appointment by 3:30.

My fifth appointment lives about 8 miles from my fourth appointment and takes me about 1 hour.

Here is another example of an easy route.

    9:00–10:00   Shih Tzu/Poodle mix
    10:00–11:00   2 Bichons
    12:00–1:00   Westie

    1:00–2:00   Yorkie
    2:00–3:00   Shih Tzu
    3:00–4:00   Shih Tzu

This is a nice day.

My first stop takes me about 1 hour.

My second stop is two Bichons that are kept in 4F all over with a traditional Bichon style head. It takes me about 1 hour and 45 minutes to groom both of them. They live about 5 miles from my first stop. I will have no problem arriving at my next stop by 12:15.

My third stop is a Westie that lives 2 miles from my second stop. She takes me 45 minutes, again a fast dryer and easy to groom. I plan on arriving to my next stop by 1:15.

My fourth stop is a Yorkie that lives in a gated community which takes me 45 minutes. She is about 3 miles from my third stop. I will arrive at my next appointment at approximately 2:15.

My fifth stop is in the same gated community about ¾ of a mile down the road and takes me 45 minutes. I will have no problem arriving to my next appointment by 3:15.

My sixth stop is also in the same gated community about ½ of a mile down the road and takes me about 45 minutes.

All of these dogs, as all my clientele, are on four to five week standing appointments. I do maintenance trims, which I discuss in the chapter In and Out with Style. You can see how quickly I get in and out of my stops. These dogs are all in stylized trims with the exception of a couple that are 4F all over. However, they are still on regular schedules. Most of the dogs are in trims with scissored legs. See Chapter 12 for tips on stylized trims.

You will notice in all three scenarios' that I allow plenty of time in case an appointment takes longer than planned. Allowing additional time within my arrival one hour window will help me catch up if I start to run behind schedule. This window also allows for me to run ahead of schedule as well.

Routing

When routing my schedule I will start my first job closest to my house. I work myself into town and then work my way back home. This doesn't always work out, but I try. I would rather start near home so I don't have to leave the house too early and drive far to get to my first stop. The least amount of time in between stops the better. There are times when I have looked at my book the night before and decided to switch people around to make my day flow better. I will call and ask, "Do you mind if I switch your time for tomorrow? I am just trying to make my route flow better." They almost always say, "Sure, no problem." People realize how expensive gas is and they are very willing to help you out.

As you start to get your clients on good schedules and get their dogs in nice trims that are working for you and the client, you will be able to route yourself much more easily.

Try not to get into the habit of booking certain clients on certain days. For example, Mrs. Smith might say, "I would like you to come on Tuesdays." This is fine for a few clients; however, if too many clients do that, you will run into a lot of conflicts when trying to map out your route. You may be in Mrs. Smith's area on Wednesday grooming several dogs and it would be so much easier to go to her house too. Instead you have to make a special trip there on Tuesday.

I ask my clients, "Are there any days that are not good for you?" They may say, "Any day is good except for Fridays." I will immediately write that on the client card so I know not to schedule them on Fridays. They may say, "Any day is good as long as it is after 2:00." Make a notation on their card for future scheduling. These things will help you route yourself without having to make changes later.

You may live in an area where you have no choice but to drive 15 minutes into town to start working. All areas are different. I know groomers who drive 30 minutes to an area and work there all day. Everyone is in a different situation. Just try to keep your route as tight as you can and don't backtrack. Driving back and forth from one area to the next is wasting precious time. Try to work out something with the client where you can get in to get the dog if they are not home.

Holidays

Holidays are a very busy time for groomers. We all like to enjoy the holiday season. In order to keep things running smoothly I will plan ahead. Once I receive my appointment book for the new year I will go through and mark off all the time I want off. I mark my days off for the holidays, vacations and trade shows that I am going to. When my kids were in grade school I would mark off all of their days off from school so I could be home with them. I then work my clients in around my schedule. In September I give my clients their holiday schedule, which consists of their November and December appointments. I do this in the event they are going away for the holiday and/or have family obligations. I want to know now so I can make changes to their schedules. This is my holiday season too and I would rather things run smoothly than overbook myself.

Vacations

In June I ask my clients if they have vacations planned for the summer. I will work their grooming appointments around their planned vacation. I prefer to take a week off in July and a week off in August, so I like to know in June what everyone is doing. If you think ahead, you will not have conflicts and your scheduling will run smoothly. If you don't think of these things, then you will end up overbooking yourself for lack of planning.

Winter Appointments

Winters can be challenging in the northern climates. It is not worth jeopardizing my vehicle when the roads are slippery with ice and snow. I will reschedule my day if I find that the roads are not safe; however, if a few inches of snow have accumulated overnight I will wait until the plows have cleared the roads and start my day an hour or so later. If it snows during the day, I will go home without a question. Grooming vans are not great in the snow, as they are very heavy and have difficulty stopping. Snow tires are a necessity in the northern climates. All-weather tires may work well in other areas of the country where the winter is not as severe.

When there is a lot of snow accumulation I think of two things: I could go out after the plows are done, but will my clients' driveways be clear? If my client did not clear the driveway, I would have to park on the street and trek through the snow to get the dog. When the streets are plowed there can be large snow banks on the side of the roads, which will prevent me from parking there safely.

I know I am a good driver in the snow, but there are a lot of adults and teenagers on the road who may not be as cautious.

Take the safe route and reschedule your entire day to your day off. It is so important not to work seven days a week so you have room for error. I would rather move an entire day of appointments to my day off rather than go out a half a day here and a half a day there.

Many times I decide whether I am going to work or not based on the school district. If the schools are closed, then that gives me good enough reason to reschedule my day. If the schools have a delayed opening, I may decide to start an hour or so late myself. People understand; they do not want to see you come out in bad weather.

Appointment Books and Appointment Software

I prefer using a Day Minder Week-At-A-Glance appointment book which I purchase at an office supply store. It shows one week at a time and has each day broken down into times from 8 a.m. to 5 p.m. in one-hour increments. It has always worked well for me. I never felt comfortable doing a computerized appointment system. It's just one of those things that I never trusted. I know many people who use Palm Pilots and scheduling software. I feel more comfortable with an appointment book.

Reminder Cards vs. Reminder Calls

I am a firm believer in reminder cards. I send out reminder cards the week prior to all appointments. Over the last 14 years I can say that people love them and rely on them. They very rarely ever missed an appointment.

I don't have time in the evening or during the day to call people to remind them of their appointment for the next day. When I get on the phone with clients I tend to chat for at least 10 to 15 minutes. When I spend 15 minutes on every call, it takes forever to get through the calls for the next day. People love to talk about their pets, which is fine, but when you have several calls to make it really takes its toll. Reminder cards eliminate this.

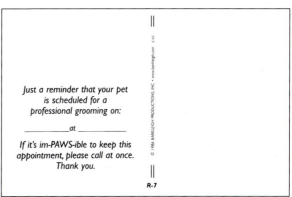

Reminder cards are great to announce a price increase. I will stick a pre-printed label on the card announcing my increase effective at the client's next visit. Barkleigh Productions has a variety of reminder cards available.

When gas prices increased to their highest that I could ever remember, I decided to cut back on my expenses. I stopped sending reminder cards, although I made sure my clients saw their next appointment that was written on their invoice. The first month without reminder cards I had many missed appointments. Some days I had up to two people miss their appointments. My clients felt so bad and told me how much they relied on the cards. Their days are hectic with kids and just life in general. When they received their reminder card they would automatically put it on their refrigerator. I know if I don't look at my calendar I tend to forget upcoming events as well. I went back to sending the cards out because the cost of the card was far less than the income I lost from clients not being home.

E-mail and Text Messaging

So many people use their e-mail on a daily basis. E-mail is a great way to remind your customers of their next appointment. This will save you money in reminder cards and stamps. However, many people are not Internet savvy, especially the elderly, so you may still want to send certain clients a card.

Most clients have cell phones, so text messaging is another way to stay in touch. Utilizing all these options will help you save money, save time and keep your schedule running smoothly.

Release Forms

You should keep release forms on file in the event of an injury or a health condition that arises when the pet is under your care. There are forms for extremely matted dogs and for elderly dogs. Shaving extremely matted dogs can be very difficult and may cause irritation, clipper burn, nicks and possible abrasions. The grooming process for elderly dogs can be very stressful. You should use a standard form that allows you to seek medical attention for a pet in the absence of the owner. These forms are used to release you from any liability in the event that anything happens during the grooming process that is out of your control. Release forms are available through Barkleigh Productions.

SENIOR PET FORM

DATE: _____

PET'S NAME: _____

Your pet is important to us. Because we care, we want to assure you that every effort will be made to make your senior pet's visit as pleasant as possible.

Occasionally, grooming can expose a hidden medical problem or aggravate a current one. This can occur during or after grooming.

In the best interest of your pet, we request your permission to obtain immediate veterinary treatment for your pet, should it become necessary.

Your Professional Groomer

I hereby grant permission to this Grooming Establishment to obtain emergency veterinary treatment for my pet. Also, realizing that Senior Pets have a greater chance of injury during grooming, I will not hold this Grooming Establishment responsible for accident or injury to my pet during the grooming procedure.

_____
Signature

#SP-1 • ©1986 Barkleigh Productions, Inc. • 717.691.3388 • www.barkleigh.com

Pet Release Form

Date: _____

Pet's Name: _____

Your Pet is important to us. Because we care, we want to assure you that every effort will be taken to make your pet's visit as pleasant as possible.

Occasionally, grooming can expose a hidden medical problem or aggravate a current one. This can occur during or after grooming.

In the best interest of your pet, we request permission to obtain immediate veterinary treatment, at your expense, should it become necessary.

I hereby grant permission to this Grooming Establishment to obtain emergency veterinary treatment for my pet, at my expense.

_____
Signature

Sincerely,
Your Professional Groomer

#PR-1 ©1986 Barkleigh Productions, Inc. • (717) 691-3388 • www.barkleigh.com   J630

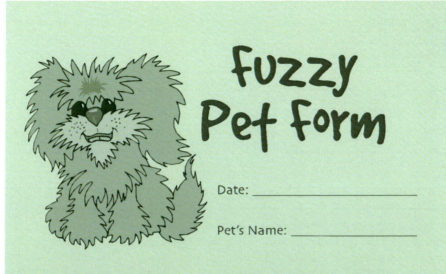

Fuzzy Pet Form

Date: _____

Pet's Name: _____

Your pet is important to us. Because we care about your pet's safety and well being, we want to assure you that every effort will be made to make your pet's visit as pleasant as possible.

Because your pet is severely tangled or matted, it is at greater risk of injury, stress and trauma. All precautions will be taken. However, problems occasionally arise, during or after grooming, such as nicks, clipper irritation and mental or physical stress.

In the best interest of your pet, we request your permission to obtain immediate veterinary treatment should it become necessary.

Sincerely,

Your Professional Groomer

I hereby grant permission to this Grooming Establishment to obtain emergency veterinary treatment for my pet at my expense. Also, realizing that matted pets have a greater chance of injury during grooming, I will not hold this Grooming Establishment responsible for accident or injury to my pet.

_____
Signature of Pet Owner

#FP-1 • ©1986 Barkleigh Productions, Inc. • 717.691.3388 • Barkleigh@aol.com   E10133

Tip to Remember:

Keep your route tight and stick to your boundary lines. Always try to have access to a clients home in the event they are not home. Once you develop trust with your client they will feel very comfortable leaving you a key or garage code. If you do not have access to their home be sure you have a cell phone number to reach them if they are not home. Allow yourself plenty of time between appointments until you develop your speed and get your clients of good schedules.

CHAPTER EIGHT

Your First Day on the Road

Filling Up

Always start the day with a full tank of gas. Generators that run off of the gas tank of the vehicle should be turned off when refueling. Once I get started with my day I don't like to take time out of my schedule to refuel. I always check to see if I have everything I need. I will check my supplies and towels and make sure my water tank is full. I never want to want to run out of water halfway through the day.

Upon Arrival

When you arrive at your first stop you will want to bring in a client card and a slip lead. When the client comes to the door the first thing that I like to do is bend down to greet the dog. Put your hand out and let the dog come to you. Then you can greet the client. There are several things you want to discuss.

- Ask who is your client's veterinarian.
- Ask if your client has an emergency number or cell phone.
- Discuss any health issues with the client.
- Check the condition of the coat while you are bending down talking to the dog. It doesn't take much to see if a dog is really matted or not.
- If the condition seems fine, ask clients what type of trim they would like.
- Ask how short or how long a cut the client wants.
- If the clients say they would like their dog to be 1 inch, show them 1 inch with your fingers to make sure that is what they want. Be clear with the clients as far as what they

are looking for. If they say they don't know, do whatever you think . . . that's great! At that point I would give them some suggestions.

If you see that the trim that they have is not suitable for that dog, don't be afraid to give them suggestions for something different. I always say, "You know what would look really cute…" Let's say that the dog is a Schnauzer and the pattern is all wrong. I would say, "Do you mind if I make some adjustments to the trim? It is a bit off and I would like to make your dog look more like a Schnauzer." People really like the fact that you care enough to make their dog look better.

If you decide to give treats, be sure you ask the clients first if their dog can have treats. If their dog has allergies or has special treats, you can bring their treats into the van to give the dog when you are done grooming.

Make notes on the client card so you have all this information. Let the dog investigate you while you are talking to the client. If the client is holding the dog, ask her or him to put the dog on the ground. I would not recommend taking the dog from the owner's arms, especially on the first visit. The dog doesn't know who you are and may become frightened.

The owners may ask to come and see your vehicle. Take them on a little tour and show them around. They will feel very comfortable knowing where their pet is going to be.

Some owners, including children, may ask to stay in the van to watch. When the owner is present the dog wants to get to the owner the entire time. The owner and the kids will constantly talk to the dog, getting the dog excited. Tell the owner that the dog will do better if they are not there. I always say that I need the dog's complete attention so no injuries occur. If the dog is jumping around trying to get to the owner, it will be very difficult to get the job done. If the owner or the child gets hurt while in your vehicle, it becomes a liability issue.

When I get the dog out to the van I immediately lock myself in. You don't want anyone opening the door unexpectedly and have the dog bolt out.

> I was grooming in a senior citizen community several years ago and all of a sudden I heard someone in my driver's seat knocking on the wall to the grooming area. It scared the daylights out of me. I opened the pass-through door and there was an old man sitting in my driver's seat! He knew I was in there but didn't know how to get in. He wanted to know if I could groom his dog.

> Another time I was grooming an old Airedale. I had just put her on the floor and I was writing out my invoice when a friend saw me and stopped by to say hello. She opened

up my door to pop her head in and the Airedale bolted out the door! What a scene that was. I had to go to the client's door and ask her to help us catch the dog. The dog was scared and just ran and ran; however, with the owner's help we finally were able to get the dog without a problem.

I now lock myself in all the time. If you have a client with multiple pets and they are all in your van, you never want to leave your doors unlocked. It is better to be safe than sorry.

Detecting Problems During Grooming

If you ever see any issues while you are grooming, whether it be fleas, hot spots, cuts or bruises or anything else that you think the owners should know about immediately, you should call them from your cell phone while you are in the van. I do this because I want them to be aware that I found something right away, especially if I see fleas. You want them to wash all the bedding while the dog is in your van. They should also vacuum the house well while you are grooming the dog.

If you see skin tags, warts, lumps or bumps, you should make notes on the client card so you remember they are there for the next time. This will prevent you from possibly nicking them in the future.

When You Are Finished

When I am finished grooming I put the dog on my floor. I write up an invoice, which allows the dog to shake and get excited to go into the house. I will praise the dog to get it feeling good about the grooming experience. I'll put the dog back up on the table for a minute to see if I need to tweak anything up. You can offer the dog a treat at that point. We are now ready to go into the house.

With small dogs I never let them jump out of the van. If a small dog tries to jump out of your van, it could stumble and before you know it the dog is limping to the door. Yes, that has happened to me. Since then I always carry small dogs down the steps and put them down on the ground. Always bring the dog back to the house on a leash. You never want to trust dogs to run back to the house, even if the owner allows them to be off leash. Remember, they really don't know you and could run from you when you get outside, or they may see a squirrel or another dog and take off after it.

Bring the invoice, a business card and your appointment book into the house with you. Ask the clients if they are happy with the trim and the length that you chose. If they are happy with the grooming, make notes on your client card with the exact blade and/or snap-on combs that you used so you will know for the next visit. If clients prefer the trim shorter or longer, be sure to make notes on the card. It is hard to remember every dog, so making notes will be very helpful at the next grooming appointment. Tell the clients how well their dog did and how cute the dog was. I then ask the clients how often would they like their dog groomed. If they say they are not sure and they will call you, explain to them how the service works.

> I will say, "Just keep in mind that I run my business on standing appointments so I can route myself easily. You should allow at least two weeks' notice for me to get you into my book. The holidays are coming [if applicable] and I will be very busy, so if you want to make an appointment now it would be best."

If they book an appointment great! If they don't, don't worry. What will happen is they will call you six weeks later and you won't be able to get them in for two weeks. Now their dog is going to be well overdue for a bath. Next time they will rebook because they will not want to wait until you can get them in. Even if it doesn't happen the second time around, it will happen very soon. People learn quickly that they should schedule an appointment if they want their dog groomed regularly.

Many times clients will ask me what I recommend for a grooming schedule. I always tell them 4 to 6 weeks is best. I explain that if they like the trim that I did, then this schedule will keep their dog looking nice without becoming matted. If they still are undecided, I would then recommend 5 weeks and say "let's see how they do on this schedule."

Clients will soon realize how convenient this service is and suddenly they will say, "What if I just leave the door open or give you my garage code in case I'm not home?" They will quickly be on regular schedules with standing appointments. If they have to think about calling and making an appointment for their dog, most of the time at that point the dog is overdue. Booking their next appointment while you are there becomes common practice.

Taking Care of Yourself

When you first start your business you are trying desperately to stay on schedule. You may want to pack yourself a lunch and drinks for the day so you don't have to stop. During the summer it is always a good idea to bring a lot of water with you and fresh fruit to keep you going throughout the day.

Parking

I always park in the customer's driveway with the doors to the grooming area at the front walk of the client's house, or as close as I can. Ask the client if it is okay to park in the driveway, especially if you see more than one car parked there. I will ask, "Does anyone have to leave while I am here?" It is very inconvenient to have to stop grooming to move your vehicle. If you have trouble seeing while backing up the vehicle, you may want to back into the driveway, which will make it easier when it comes time to leave your appointment. Backing up into traffic from a client's driveway can be difficult with some of the larger model conversions.

If the driveway is not level, I prefer to park on the street. It can be difficult to groom in a driveway that has too much pitch.

Grooming Multiple Pets

When a client has more than one dog it is a good idea to take them all in the van at the same time. If they are two large breeds it may be harder to do that depending upon the space limitations of your vehicle. I find that if I have to go back and forth to get the dogs one at a time I end up wasting time talking to the owner each time I go back to the house. I prefer to do it this way so I can have one dog washed and drip drying while I am washing and drying the second dog. I always try to use my time wisely.

> I have three Cocker Spaniels at one stop. I take them all in and do the clipperwork on all three dogs first. I wash one, towel dry really well, and HV dry him to get the water off and separate the coat. I then sit him on a towel on my table with my stand dryer blowing on him. I now wash the second dog, towel dry, and HV dry him. I go back to the dog on the table and move the stand dryer to the dog in the tub and HV the dog on the table all the way dry, ready for grooming. I move this dog to the floor and put the dog that is in the tub on my table. I put the stand dryer on him and put the third dog in the tub and wash. I towel dry and HV dry him and move the stand dryer on him while I finish drying the dog on the table. I put the dog on the table on the floor and finish drying the dog in the tub.
>
> Now all three dogs are ready for their haircuts. Whenever you have one dog on the grooming table and one dog in the tub, you always should be within arm's reach and have the dogs in grooming loops. I never turn my back on the dogs. I can bathe the one dog facing to the side where I can see the dog on the table right next to me. Accidents can happen quickly, so always think safety first.

By doing this the dogs are getting partially dry while I am working on the other dogs. This way I am not drying the dogs from dripping wet, which takes longer. I can get out of this stop in 2 hours and 30 minutes.

When I have two little dogs at one stop I will always wash them together and dry them together which saves me a lot of time. I find that they also feel secure because they are together.

Fleas

If you ever see fleas on a dog you want to call the owner immediately and tell them, as discussed above. I charge a fee for flea shampoo and flea clean-up. I always carry a natural flea shampoo and a premise spray in my vehicle. When I am finished with that appointment I will spray my vehicle down keeping the vents/windows open to ventilate. I have even cancelled my entire day due to a dog with fleas. The last thing I want to do is bring fleas to my next appointment. When returning to a customer who I know had fleas last month I always use a flea shampoo again just in case there is still a problem.

If clients or potential clients call and tell you that they are having a flea problem, I would not recommend scheduling an appointment just yet. They must treat their pet with Advantix or whatever other product they choose to use. Once the dog is treated they can call me back. I explain to them the nature of my business. Due to the fact that I go to clients' homes, I cannot service someone who has a flea infestation. I take flea infestations very seriously, and don't want to pass them along to other clients or bring them home to my dogs.

Skunk Odor

I treat skunk attacks and flea infestations in the same manner. I never take a freshly sprayed dog into my van; otherwise it will smell like skunk for days. I always tell people to wash their dog immediately in a solution of 1/4 cup of baking soda, one quart of 3% hydrogen peroxide and 2 tablespoons of any dish soap, such as Joy soap. The key to using this mixture is to mix it vigorously until it becomes foamy. This is when it works best. Once the mixture sits and loses the foam it will not do its job. This mixture should stay on the coat for 15 minutes or more, being careful not to get it in the eyes. Most likely the dogs are sprayed in the face and chest. If this is the case, I will focus on those areas and not wash the entire dog in this solution. Once the clients do the initial bath I will then schedule an appointment. I always keep these bath supplies on hand. If skunk oil is not washed off immediately, it is difficult to get the smell out.

At the End of the Day

At the end of the day, drain the grey tank. You can do this in your driveway at home. The shampoo that we use is biodegradable and non-toxic, so it is not harmful to the environment. This soapy water is no different from water from washing your car. Dirty water contains nitrogen, which is beneficial to plants and vegetation and which will promote growth. Many groomers use this water to water their shrubs and flowers.

Wash the tub out and clean the van really well so tomorrow you will get into a nice clean van. I clean up in between every groom and save the big clean-up for the end of the day.

I will now check my blades to see if they need oil, empty my garbage and vacuum so I am ready for another day.

Tip to Remember:

Always leave your home in the morning on time so your day will run smoothly. Use your time wisely throughout the day. First impressions mean everything. Present yourself and your business in a professional manner. If you love what you do, you will never work a day in your life!

CHAPTER NINE

Managing Your Clientele

Loyalty

When your business becomes established and clients have standing appointments you will notice that your clients become very loyal to you. They will recommend your services to friends and family. They will even brag about your service to their veterinarian. I enjoy all my clients and have developed great relationships with them. I am just as loyal to them as they are to me.

> One time I had this little Maltese that was in full coat. He had a nice ponytail. It was Easter weekend and I had just been there grooming him during the week. I tied up his ponytail with a really cute Easter bow. Saturday night came and my client could not get the bow in, so she called me to ask how I did it. She lived in the gated community that I spoke about earlier. I told her I would be right over. She was just shocked that I would come out on a Saturday night to put a bow in her dog's hair. Well, she was only a few miles from my house and it was not a big deal. After that night she showered me with gifts for every occasion. She also tipped me very well at every visit.

Loyalty to your clients goes a long way. Do for them and they will do for you. My grandmother always said, "Treat people the way you want to be treated."

When A Pet Passes Away

It is always sad to see our four-legged customers pass away. Be sure to send out sympathy cards. Your clients will most likely replace their pet at some point, so make sure you always save a spot in your book for them.

Newsletters

Newsletters are a great form of communication between you and your clients. My clients enjoyed reading of my achievements in the grooming industry. I also took the time to recognize the dogs that passed away over the year. Newsletters also gave me an opportunity to let people know the services that I offer as well as the retail that I carry. It is hard when you are mobile to sell products and services, so I felt this was a great way to make announcements. I prefer to send my newsletters in the spring, which gives me an opportunity to talk about flea/tick products, vacation schedules, price increases, and so on. I would also take the time to thank my clients for their business throughout the year. I called it "The Puppy Spa News."

Holiday Gifts

It is always nice to give clients gifts for their dog for the holidays. Here are some things that I liked to do over the years.

> One year I brought small Ziploc bags to work with me along with a Sharpie. I started collecting locks of hair from the dogs and put them in bags with each dog's name on its bag. I started doing this in September. I bought clear glass Christmas balls from the craft store. I tied each little lock of hair with a skinny Christmas ribbon and placed it in the ball. I wrote my business name and year with fabric paint that worked on glass on one side and on the other side I wrote the dog's name. These were great keepsakes and everyone really liked them.

> I have a little pet bakery store in town that bakes doggie cookies from scratch. The store owner is also a client of mine. She makes fabulous cookies in all shapes and sizes. I have her make me up a little bag of cookies with about five nice-size cookies per bag. She may include a gingerbread man, a Christmas tree, a star and so on. They were wrapped in clear cute bags and tied up with a ribbon. I also buy toys and give everyone a little toy and a bag of cookies.

> Another time I bought little stockings at the craft store. I had my daughter sit and write every dog's name on a stocking in glitter. I filled each stocking with cute little toys, chews and cookies.

> I have also taken pictures of the dogs when they are getting a bath or after they are groomed and frame them in holiday frames.

> I always buy Hanukkah cookies and toys for customers as well.

Maintaining Your Client Base

Mobile groomers fill their client base very quickly. Keep track of how many clients you are taking on. When working five days per week while grooming six dogs per day you will only need approximately 120 clients if they are on a four week schedule.

When working five days per week while grooming six dogs per day that are on a six week schedule, then you can take on approximately 180 clients.

Taking on too many clients can create scheduling issues and unhappy clients. If someone wants to book an appointment in four weeks and you find that you have no openings, you may have taken on too many clients. Scheduling clients for three appointments will allow for you to see what the availability is for adding new clients. Having one appointment at a time in your book makes it difficult to tell if you have openings for new clients.

I have never taken on more than 130 dogs. I work four days per week with the majority of my clients on four to five week schedules. I have several dogs that are on a two week schedule as well. Keep yourself in a comfortable place where you will continue to enjoy your business and not feel overwhelmed.

I avoid grooming the once-a-year dogs, since they are not maintained regularly. These dogs are usually in very bad condition and are very time-consuming. They are not accustomed to the grooming process and can be difficult to groom. Once your business becomes established you will not be able to take on this type of customer, which is why I recommend not taking them on in the beginning.

Your goal should be to get everyone on standing appointments. I give appointments out at every visit. There is not one dog that I groom that is not in my book on an ongoing basis.

Most mobile groomers are booked solid within six months of starting up their business. It happens very quickly. This doesn't mean that this will be your clientele forever. Clients may come and go. You may even let people go who are just not working out for you. It will take up to a year to really get the clientele that will most likely stay with you for a long time.

The best thing about mobile grooming is that you can be very selective as to what breeds you take on. If you only need 120 to 180 clients, then why not make them the breeds you want to do? Some groomers only want to groom small dogs, where other groomers love to groom large breeds. If you prefer not to groom Bernese Mountain Dogs, German Shepherds, Old English Sheepdogs, Keeshonds, Malamutes, and similar breeds, then don't do them. The large breeds can be hard to maneuver. They can be difficult to get into the bathtub, especially by yourself. I groom Golden

Retrievers, Setters, Standard Poodles and Portuguese Water Dogs, yet I prefer not to groom the larger breeds. Everyone has their own specialty. The Golden Retrievers, Labs, Shelties, Pointers and similar breeds give me a break from scissoring and I really enjoy grooming them.

Cats are also a great money maker if you are a cat groomer. There are not many cat groomers around, so people are always searching for them. See Chapter 10 on Grooming Cats in a Mobile Unit.

Fine-tuning Your Clientele

After you have been in business for one year it is time to take a good look at your route. Are you driving in circles? Are you driving to areas that you really don't need to travel to anymore? It's time to fine-tune your route. If you decide that you are driving too far, then you may want to start cutting back those clients. Explain to them that you are not servicing their area any longer. It is always nice to refer them to another groomer if you can. At this point you can start taking on more clients in your most prominent areas.

Try to get clients who live near each other on the same schedule. If Mrs. Cook and Mrs. Brown both have dogs that are on five week schedules and live in the same neighborhood, yet one is scheduled for this week and one is scheduled for next week, you can make modifications that will allow you to groom both dogs the same week. You may have to let one client go to a six week schedule instead of a five week schedule one time just to get them in sync.

Look at your clientele. Are there dogs that you just don't enjoy grooming? Do you have customers whom you just can't seem to please? It's time to let them go. Sometimes our personalities just don't mix with certain dogs. I remember my friend who owns a shop told me that one of her groomers has a heck of a time with certain dogs, yet those same dogs do great for her. If you have dogs that you just can't seem to control, then don't feel bad about letting them go. If your phone is ringing on a regular basis, you can feel confident that you can replace these dogs with new dogs that you will enjoy more.

A great time to increase prices is when you take on new customers. Bring them in at a higher rate than when you started last year.

Fine-tuning your route and your clientele will end up making you more money and will keep your job enjoyable. I have let several clients go over the years because of stress. You cannot please everyone.

> I had a little Maltese that the owner insisted on keeping in full coat to the ground. He was older and his hair was very fine. It was very easy to keep. I groomed him every four weeks. He became sick and passed away, at which time the owner bought a puppy. We all know what puppy coat can be like. His coat was very much like cotton and wasn't anything like their other dog. He just looked like a fluffy marshmallow. When he turned about a year old he went through a horrible coat change and he was matting very badly. The owner carried him around all the time and you could see where she held him. The one entire side of him was a matted mess. I tried all my tricks of the trade to try to keep him from matting, yet nothing seemed to work. I even had them put all his dog beds in satin pillowcases. I changed their schedule from 4 weeks to every 2 weeks and he was still matting. They couldn't brush him because he would bite them. I finally told them that they had to decide if they wanted to keep him long or cut him back. If they kept him long I told them I would have to come every week; otherwise we needed to cut him down. Over that one-year period I developed tennis elbow. I started to notice that it would flare up every time I de-matted him, and I had to have cortisone shots to ease the pain. The owner insisted on keeping him long so I had no choice but to bathe him every week. I noticed the owner was getting annoyed and

wasn't as pleasant as she had been in the past. She was obviously upset that I insisted on weekly appointments. I finally called her one day and told her that I would not be able to groom her dog any longer. I told her that I felt she was unhappy and that she should find another groomer. I was very nice about it and explained to her that I was having issues with my elbow. She was really mad that I was letting her go; however, I felt a huge sigh of relief when I made that decision. I never have had another shot of cortisone and have not had another flare-up of my tennis elbow. All of that developed from de-matting this dog.

There are many dogs out there to add to your clientele, so don't feel as though you have to keep the difficult dogs/clients just because.

Tip to Remember:

The holiday season is a great time to show your clients how much you appreciate their business. Be prepared for the holidays by scheduling appointments in advance. Always keep track of your client base so your business will run smoothly. Letting go clients that you do not enjoy grooming is not a bad thing. It's just difficult to do sometimes. Aways remember that it is a business decision.

CHAPTER TEN

Grooming Cats in a Mobile Unit

Cats are not, by nature, very outgoing and adaptable to new situations. Cats can become stressed rather easily. And too much stress on an elderly cat or one with certain underlying health issues can have disastrous results. For these reasons, providing a quiet, stress-free environment during the grooming process should be of utmost importance. Mobile grooming does just that and a whole lot more!

Cats are also notoriously poor travelers. They often meow, cry, potty, and vomit during car rides. Most felines hate leaving the comforts of their own home to go anywhere, much less take a trip to the local grooming salon. Because mobile grooming eliminates travel in a car and the accompanying stress, it is ideal for many felines. Many mobile groomers have a virtually untapped market right outside their van doors and are doing little, if nothing, to capitalize on it.

Marketing and Soliciting New Cat Clients

Statics show that there are more owned cats in the United States than there are dogs. This means that every household a mobile groomer visits for the purposes of grooming the family canine is likely also to have a cat or two.

To take advantage of these furry little potential clients, a groomer needs to take these steps.

1. Get the word out.

If no one knows that I groom cats, how will they buy my services? You should do some form of marketing or advertising to let existing and potential clients know that you are a mobile groomer who offers specialized cat grooming services. Announcing this on your mobile unit itself is a good idea. In addition, you should make some mention of cats on your website, business cards, brochures and other advertising material. Ask about the cats in the client's household and offer grooming services that are appropriate for each cat. Point out the "issues" that are obvious (excessive shedding, hairballs, matting, dandruff, torn furniture from sharp claws, and so on) and offer real solutions.

The National Cat Groomers Institute of America, Inc. (NCGIA) offers client brochures designed specifically for the purpose of soliciting new cat-owning clientele. The brochures are called "A Groomed Cat Is a Happy Cat" and "Got Hairballs?" Both can be ordered in packs of 50 or 100 and provide space on the outer panel to list your contact information. In addition, the NCGIA also offers a set of 7 marketing posters that point out various issues that cats and their owners may be dealing with due to nonexistent or infrequent grooming of the cat. While posters are not always suited to a mobile environment, you could ask to post them at veterinarian offices or other places of referral.

2. Dispel the myths about cat grooming.

Most people believe that cats groom themselves. Cats do not "groom" themselves, they lick themselves, which deposits saliva and dander containing the allergen protein Fel-d-1 throughout their coat.

Dispelling the myths means pointing out the reality of the situation. Cats suffer from shedding, hairballs, mats, tangles, dandruff, dander, overgrown nails, dirty ears, greasy coats, foul odors, tear staining and more, yet they are helpless to do anything about it. They need the help and expertise of a professional cat groomer.

Examples of matted, pelted cat, a pelt shaved off a Himalayan.

Another myth about cats and grooming is that cats hate water. This is simply not true. Most cats tolerate water fairly well and are glad to have had a good bath and blow dry. In fact, some of the most aggressive cats can be handled without too much difficulty once they are soaking wet. For more on the effects of water on aggressive cats, check out the NCGIA's "Kryptonite for Cats" DVD.

3. Make it happen.

If a groomer is already in the driveway, grooming the dog, why not throw in a cat or two? Talk the owner into trying out the offered cat grooming services. Proof is in the pudding, as they say. That means the finished results need to be amazing and truly make a difference for the owner and the cat. Prove what benefits there are to professional cat grooming, and particularly mobile cat grooming, which eliminates the unnecessary stresses associated with travel and being in a noisy, non-cat-exclusive environment. Once clients see the remarkable difference a quality cat groom can make, they will most likely be happy to rebook the kitties along with the dog for the next appointment.

Before

After

Pricing

There is definitely good money to be made when it comes to cat grooming, especially mobile cat grooming. A good cat groomer should be able to finish cats in a fast, efficient manner, thus providing for more cats groomed per day than the average number of dogs that can be completed.

Cat grooming is also a very specialized service. Not everyone does it. Not many are cut out for it. And not many are willing to give it a try. Less competition means less supply and more demand, which in turn means higher prices.

Before

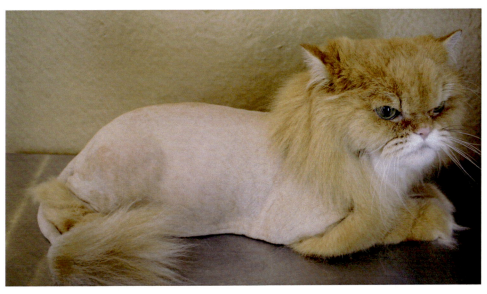

After

NCGIA certified mobile cat groomers tend to average approximately $145 per cat. Using the formula on the weekly and monthly income amounts can be estimated for the four day work week.

$145 per cat average
Groom 8 cats per day = $1160 per day
$1160 x 4 days per week = $4640 per week
$4640 per week x 4 weeks = $18,560 per month

Using the same overhead expenses as previously shown, the estimated profit would be as follows:

$18,560 per month – $2,000 (average expenses) = $16,560 profit per month
$16,560 divided by 16 days per month (4 days per week) = $1,035 per day profit
$16,560 x 12 months = $198,720 per year profit!!

The five day work week would look like this:

$145 per cat average
Groom 8 cats per day = $1160 per day
$1160 x 5 days per week = $5800 per week
$5800 per week x 4 weeks = $23,200 per month

$23,200 per month –$2,000 (average expenses) = $21,200 profit per month
$21,200 divided by 20 days per month (5 days per week) = $1,060 per day profit
$21,200 x 12 months = $254,400 per year profit!!

These figures are based on average mobile cat grooming prices in the United States. Not all cats will incur a charge of $145. However, some may incur a higher or lower charge based on service, condition, or other factors. Also, speed and efficiency certainly contribute to the number of cats that you can groom in a day. Good handling skills and a thorough understanding of cat temperaments and behaviors are vital in working quickly, safely, and efficiently. Until you have gained those particular skills and the accompanying knowledge, the number of cats you can groom in one day may be less. On the other hand, if you have a healthy clientele load and can work efficiently with cats, you may be able to increase the daily number.

Extra Fees

You should charge extra handling fees for overly aggressive cats and those in bad condition. Examples are:

Severely matted cats
Cats with hair matted into a thick pelt
Cats with excessive fecal matter stuck in their coat
Flea-infested cats

Highly aggressive cats, especially those in bad condition, as the aggression only becomes worse due to the severity of matting/pelting.

In addition, you should charge a handling fee whenever you must locate and catch the cat prior to grooming it.

Collecting and Transporting the Cat

No one wants to chase a cat around the house, trying to catch it when it doesn't want to be caught. A chased cat is usually an angry cat. And felines tend to notice very quickly when things are out of the ordinary. It is not uncommon for a cat to disappear at the sight of its carrier or crate. When the carrier appears, it means a trip to the vet's or the groomer's. Most cats are quick to avoid either one.

Instruct cat owners to collect their cat well before the scheduled appointment time. They should place their cat in a bathroom or other small room until just before the appointment time. The room should be free of beds, large furniture pieces or other cubbyholes and hiding spots to which it can run. This makes the cat easy to find and retrieve when it is needed. Then, just before you arrive for the appointment, the owner should take the carrier or crate into the bathroom or other small room where the cat is being held and safely put the cat inside, making sure the doors and hinges are all securely fastened. The cat will then be ready for you to pick it up and carry it out to your mobile unit.

Time is money. This means that the owner should compensate you monetarily for time you spend searching for or attempting to capture the cat. You should never have to crawl under a client's bed or dig through a closet to catch a cat. In addition to the time-wasting aspects of this scenario, it is also more likely that a cat will be stressed because of it, which puts you at greater risk of being bitten or scratched during the grooming process.

Start out in the very beginning by communicating these specific instructions and requirements for collecting a cat at the time of the groom appointment. Emphasize that the cat needs to be safely and securely housed in a carrier or crate that you can easily transport to your mobile unit. Carrying a loose cat should never be an option. There is simply too much risk of a cat escaping and running away. Just about anything can startle or frighten a feline, sending it off down the street to be hit by a car or something equally tragic. Do not assume this liability. Make it a requirement that all felines be ready and waiting in an appropriate carrier at the appointed time. Transport the cat to and from your mobile unit only while it is securely housed in the carrier. Keep your mobile grooming unit's doors locked at all times when handling a cat. Do not let the cat outside the carrier until it is safely back in the owner's house and all outside doors are shut.

If a client does not abide by these requirements, then refuse the groom until the requirements are met. Charge a fee for a missed appointment, since you incurred costs (time and gas) but the groom was not performed due to the owner's non-compliance. It is for the good of the cat and the good of your business that these requirements exist.

Assessing Temperament and Condition

When you enter the client's home, the cat should be ready and waiting in a carrier or crate. You should always do a temperament and condition assessment on every new cat to determine what behavior traits you will encounter during the grooming session and what elements of grooming you can and should perform on a given cat.

Cats can be classified by temperament into three categories: shy, compliant and aggressive. It is important to understand each of the three temperament types as well as to be able to identify them during handling and grooming.

Temperament, age, health, skin and coat condition and preferences of the owner should all factor in to what you choose for a particular cat's grooming. You can assess all these things very quickly by observing the cat in its carrier and then handling the cat briefly while still in the owner's home, prior to the groom. At this point, you can discuss with the owner any recommendations, options and choices that are best for the cat.

For specific instructions for a temperament and condition assessment and further explanation of temperament types, please see *The Ultimate Cat Groomer Encyclopedia* and the NCGIA's *Temperaments and Handling Skills Study Packet*.

Products, Tools and Equipment

Time is of the essence when grooming cats. Because of this, high-quality grooming results are often sacrificed. But one does not have to be at the expense of the other. Efficiency and quality can be achieved simultaneously. The products, tools and equipment that you use can determine whether this happens or not.

Cat grooming must-haves by Danelle German:

    Air Muzzle®
    Catty Shack Vac™
    F&T Shampoo (slightly diluted)
    Hypoallergenic shampoo (slightly diluted)
    Groomer's Goop
    Flea shampoo (labeled safe for cats—do NOT use shampoo containing permethrin!)
    Clipper with #10 blade
    Mini or Pro LT trimmer®
    Clipper with Clipper Vac® attachment and #30 blade
    Romani Clipper Vac®
    Rake-N-Vac® and the Shorty Rake-N-Vac®
    Small nail trimmers
    Soft Paws® nail caps
    4 ½" blunt-tip face scissors
    7 ½" fine/medium greyhound comb
    Chris Christensen face/feet comb (available at Cherrybrook)
    Chris Christensen cat comb (available at Cherrybrook)
    Rubbing alcohol
    Renu saline solution
    Cotton balls and Q-tips
    Styptic powder
    Cat-a-tonic finishing spray

Catty Shack Vac™ in a mobile unit

Rebooking and Frequency of Grooms

On average cats should be groomed every six weeks. Some may require more frequent grooming, while others may go for a longer period in between grooming sessions while still maintaining good skin and coat condition.

It is up to you, the groomer, to determine the proper frequency for an individual cat based on its coat type, age, health and general condition. If correctly done, a cat will be completely de-greased and the coat thoroughly dried during the grooming process. The proper frequency of grooms will mean that a cat's coat stays in a mat-free condition in between grooming sessions.

It is important to effectively communicate to the owner how regular grooming can significantly improve a cat's coat and skin condition, and thus its quality of life. Conversely, allowing a cat to become matted and in poor condition creates unnecessary stress on the cat, which can lead to serious problems and even death.

Sedation

Sometimes it may be in the best interest of a cat for it to be mildly sedated before it is groomed. A groomer should never administer the sedative or any other medication to a cat. If sedation is required, instruct the owner to give the medication approximately 15 to 30 minutes before the scheduled appointment time. This will provide sufficient time for the sedative to begin working. Most sedatives will wear off approximately 90 minutes after being administered. If you are not comfortable with grooming a mildly sedated animal, then discuss your concerns with the owner.

Training and Certification

The National Cat Groomers Institute of America, Inc., headquartered in Greenville, South Carolina, and founded in 2007, is the first association for cat groomers. The NCGIA set the standards for cat grooming within the pet grooming industry when previously none existed. Today the NCGIA maintains the highest level of quality and a strong leadership position within the industry by offering the most complete training and certification to cat groomers around the globe.

The National Cat Groomers School was opened in January 2010 for the express purpose of training those within the industry who want to learn the art of cat grooming or better their existing cat grooming skills. Certification is awarded to those who pass the nine required exams that include both written and practical testing.

For more information on becoming certified through the NCGIA, visit the website at www.nation-alcatgroomers.com.

Danelle German, CFMG, CFCG, owned CFA's Bara Cattery from 1999-2005. During that time she produced and showed many National and Regional award winning Persians, including CFA's 3rd Best Cat in Premiership in 2005. Danelle is a member of Foothills Felines Cat Club, serving as President and Show Manager for a number of years. In 2005, she retired from showing to focus on her feline-exclusive spa and resort, The Catty Shack, Ltd., located in Simpsonville, SC.

Danelle is the founder of the National Cat Groomers Institute of America, Inc. and, in 2009 sold her grooming salon so she could open the world's first feline-exclusive grooming school located in Greenville, SC. She currently serves as President and Certifier/Instructor of the NCGIA and Director of the National Cat Groomers School and is a member of Wahl's X-Treme Groom Team. Along with her husband, Michael, she is the inventor and patent holder of the Catty Shack Vac™ drying system.

Danelle has authored the Ultimate Cat Groomer Encyclopedia as well as several articles for a variety of grooming publications. She is also the author of certification study guides for cat groomers and has written updated cat grooming study material for other associations. Danelle has appeared on Animal Planet's Cats 101 and Must Love Cats and has been interviewed and filmed numerous times for Discovery Channel, local TV stations, Kittens USA and other media. She is the winner of the first Groomers Got Talent competition held at Groom Expo in 2009 and has won each creative dog grooming competition that she has been allowed to compete in with a cat.

Speaking regularly on all topics related to cat grooming and behavior, Danelle is a true pioneer in the field of feline grooming. Her lectures and training materials can found around the world. In addition to speaking, Danelle has judged cat grooming competitions at various shows in both the US and Europe and has served as a judge for the Cat Writer's Association.

Tip to Remember:

There are not many certified cat groomers in the United States. In fact, there are many groomers that do not groom cats at all. Cat grooming will increase your income tremendously. Do not be afraid to charge what your service is worth.

CHAPTER ELEVEN

Managing Your Mobile Vehicle

Mobile Grooming Tips

I prefer to keep two clippers handy. I use one for snap-on combs and the second clipper for other blades. This saves me time from changing blades throughout the day. I use my Andis Excel 5-Speed clipper and the Andis Super 2-Speed daily. They are very quiet clippers and require minimal maintenance. It is also a good idea to have a cordless clipper to use on pads and sanitary trims. If you ever run into a problem with power you always can finish up with a cordless clipper. There have often been times when I have had to bring my clipper into the client's house for one reason or another. It is a tool that is very convenient to own.

When using two clippers in a mobile van the cords tend to tangle together. The Monkey Cord is a great product that prevents the clipper cord from tangling and also prevents two cords from becoming intertwined. The Monkey Cord is easy to install on any clipper cord and comes in several colors. It is available through Shear Mobility.

Carry a large golf-type umbrella with you. When it is raining you don't want the dogs to get wet on the way into the house after they have been freshly groomed. I always wear a raincoat on rainy days so I can tuck those little dogs under my coat. Clients who have larger breeds will often open their garage door so I can run their dog in quickly without getting wet. In that case, I try to park as close to the garage as possible.

Safety should always be a priority. Always have the dogs in a grooming loop on your table and in the bathtub. Never turn your back on a dog unattended.

Never leave a dog on your table or in the tub and leave your van, even for a second. Sometimes you may have a situation where you have to get to your breaker box or fuse box, which are normally located in the back of your vehicle. Always put the dog on the floor before leaving the vehicle.

I was at a client's house once and I had to go outside to check my generator. The dog I was grooming was a Spitz mix. He was a fairly good-sized dog, probably about 65 pounds. I put him on the floor and left the van for a minute. He jumped up on the door as I left to see where I went and pushed down the door lock with his paw. I just about died! I was in my own neighborhood just about a block from my house. I had my youngest son, who was about seven years old, ride his bike over. I put the owner's garbage can up next to my truck and opened the window so my son could crawl through and unlock the door. He saved the day and went to school the next day and told his teacher! I now always keep my keys in my pocket.

If you ever quick a nail and you have a hard time stopping the bleeding, it is a good idea to give your client a bit of quick stop. I had a situation once when a dog started running around the living room and knocked the quick stop off and the nail started to bleed everywhere. I was so embarrassed. I felt so bad. I always trim nails first just in case I hit a quick. This way I will have time to get the bleeding to stop. I hardly ever quick nails because I am always afraid that this will happen again. You can also tell your client they can use flour, cornstarch or pancake mix if they do not have quick stop on hand.

Condensation may build up on your windows while you are bathing the dogs. If this happens it is a good idea to open your vents and/or windows to let the condensation out. Too much moisture will prevent the dogs from drying quickly. This usually happens during the winter when it is warmer in the van than outside and also on rainy days due to the humidity level being too high. Too much moisture in the van is not good for your blades either. You may see your blades start to rust, even though they shouldn't. Place a towel over your blades at night to prevent moisture buildup and keep them properly oiled.

If you have a client who likes to talk a lot when you are done grooming, you may want to bring your cell phone into the house with you. I have called friends and told them to call me in 10 minutes. This way you can get out of there without being rude. I do this in extreme cases where I know I have a hard time getting back to my van. Sometimes I just have to tell the client that I am running a little behind, so I have to run.

Hand sanitizers work really well after you express anal glands. It takes the odor out completely.

Moisture Magnet towels rapidly absorb water out of dogs' coats. You can twist them to ring out the excess water and reuse them on the same dog. They are fabulous and I highly recommend them. While I am drying the dogs I sit them on the towel and it really absorbs water nicely. They cut down your laundry size substantially compared to regular towels. They are available through M.D.C. Romani.

The Happy Hoodie is a great product that will calm a dog during the drying process. This "head band" protects the dog's ears, which diminishes the noise and airflow that often aggravate the pet. This will allow you to get through the majority of the drying without too much fuss. I find that pets that don't like the drying process do better if I use a stand dryer on their heads instead of the HV dryer to finish them. If you don't have a stand dryer, you can also use a human hair dryer on a low heat setting. The Happy Hoodie is available through M.D.C. Romani.

It is always important to inform clients of any health condition that you may see when grooming their dog. You may even notice hair loss or that the dog is just not him/herself. We as groomers are the first to notice things out of the ordinary. However, we should never diagnose a situation. Even if you feel strongly that the dog may be suffering from a condition, you always should recommend that the owner bring the dog to their vet.

There are times when you are clippering faces, clippering Poodle feet or even scissoring near faces that dogs tend to lick at the wrong time. If you ever nick a tongue, you can put sugar on the nick and it normally stops the bleeding pretty quickly. I keep sugar packets in my first-aid drawer for this.

If you ever cut a dog you always want to tell the owners. Using vet glue can be dangerous. I have seen cuts become very infected from groomers using glue without cleaning the wound properly. Always tell the owners; they understand that accidents happen.

Peroxide on a cotton ball will remove blood from the coat almost instantly.

You may run into a situation where a dog has had to be lightly sedated for the grooming process. Many pet owners will get a prescription from their vet and sedate their dogs before they take them to the groomer. The dog may be very aggressive or just have issues with the grooming process in general. If a customer asks you to sedate their dog, you always want to say no. Never administer any sedative to any animal. I have groomed dogs that the owners have sedated before and have found that it really is a liability. I have had several animals do fine, but I had one experience that changed the way that I felt about it.

> I had a little Shih Tzu that I had been grooming for years. She was always very good. As she got older she became senile. Over time the senility became worse and worse. It started when she would scream when I turned the dryer on. I didn't realize what was happening with her until it got progressively worse. I felt so bad for her and spent so much time trying to get through the drying process. Over the summer I took her outside to let her air dry because I couldn't put the dryer on her at all. She got to the point where she wouldn't let me near her face. The owner talked to the vet and the vet agreed to give her a sedative. It did help the situation and she let me get through the next groom; however, the next appointment she began having labored breathing and was extremely lethargic. I thought she was going to die on my table. I told the owner that I couldn't groom her any more. I recommended that she have her groomed at her vet's office where she could be monitored while under sedation. It really scared me and I felt bad letting her go; however, I knew it was the right thing to do. I really loved that little dog and groomed her for six years until she become completely senile…poor thing.

It is best not to take on these cases. Refer them to a veterinarian with a groomer on staff. It is too much of a liability, not to mention how horrible we would feel if a dog died under our care.

I always bring the dog to my van and back to the house on a slip lead. I never allow a dog to run free unless they are on an electric fence and they are wearing their collar. Make sure your vehicle is within the fence line so the dog does not get zapped.

I had a couple of experiences with electric fence collars.

> My van was outside the fence line, so I took the collar off of the dog. I had it in my hand as I was going out to the truck with the dog, and as I crossed the line it zapped my hand really badly! Oouuccchhh! I never did that again. I always leave the collar with the owner now.
>
> I was at a customer's house once where I had to park on the street. The owner had two dogs, a Cocker and a Schnauzer. When I was finished I brought the Schnauzer over the fence line and put her collar on. When I went back to my truck to get the Cocker, the Schnauzer followed me and got zapped. She was screaming bloody murder! I felt sooooo bad. After that I left the collars with the owner and I brought the dogs back to the house on a lead and let her put the collars back on.

Keep in mind that some dogs may hesitate walking over the line in fear that they will get zapped. In this case you may have to carry them.

Mobile Vehicle Tips

If you have a vehicle with a generator that runs off your gas tank, most of the time you must not allow your gas tank to reach down to a quarter of a tank; otherwise your generator will stall. If you allow this to happen while you are in the middle of a groom, a quick fix is to position your truck somewhere in the driveway or street (if possible) with the front of your truck on an uphill slant. This will allow the gas in the tank to move to the back of the tank where the feeder line is to your generator. It will buy you enough time for you to get done with your appointment. Some driveways have a pitch at the bib near the street. If you are lucky you'll have a driveway with some pitch. If you can't find any pitch, then you will have to plug in to get through your appointment.

Always carry a spare water pump in your tool box. They are very easy to replace. You never want to get stuck without water.

If you have a generator, always keep oil on hand for it.

Keep a water hose in the back of the vehicle in case you run out of water. This is especially necessary during the winter months. Hoses freeze in the winter in northern climates, so even if your client had a hose outside it would probably be frozen and you would not be able to use it. Keep in mind that most homeowners turn their outdoor spigots off during the winter. If you think you may run out of water during the day, you can always stop at a gas station. They usually have water spigots available.

I use quick connects on my hose and my water fill line to my vehicle. You can purchase these at any hardware store or home improvement store. It is a quick way to connect your hose without screwing the hose into your vehicle. This is especially convenient during the winter months when it is bitter cold out.

Be aware of your vehicle height. You may come across a bridge or railroad trestle that may be too close for comfort. I have one bridge in town that is about 3 inches taller than my van. It is an old stone railroad trestle that I really don't trust. I never had the nerve to go through it. It was really inconvenient because I always had to drive out of the way to go to my appointments to avoid this bridge. Also keep in mind that most fast-food drive-thru windows have limited clearance. The only fast-food restaurant that I could go through was Wendy's.

Before leaving a stop always make sure everything is put away and tied down. Check the caps on the gallons of shampoo if you have them in your bathtub. I have lost many of gallons of shampoo over the years by forgetting to put the tops on. One time I left the gallon of shampoo on my towel bin with the lid off. I completely forgot it was there. I started driving down the road and all of a sudden I smelled this very strong scent of shampoo. I looked behind me and it was flowing all over my floor! I was on a two-lane narrow road and cars were behind me. I couldn't pull over for what seemed like forever. When I was finally able to pull over, the shampoo was all over the floor and into the step going out the door. I got out of the van and went around to the door to get into the grooming area. The shampoo was flowing out of my van. I just wanted to die. I had to cancel the rest of my day and go home to get all this shampoo off the floor. It took me forever to clean up.

Grooming vans are very heavy with the weight bearing on the rear axles. Normally the grey and fresh tanks are located in the rear of the vehicle. Some vehicles have the generator in the back as well. It is important to have your tires rotated every 4 to 5 months so you can get the most wear out of your tires. I made it a point to have the tires rotated every time the vehicle went in for a regular service.

Many vehicles build their interior walls out of aluminum, formica or other washable surface. I use dry-erase markers to make notes on the wall in an inconspicuous place. You can also make notes about your schedule for that day, record emergency phone numbers and even jot down notes from an incoming call. If you are not sure what your walls are made of, you may want to try this in a small area first. Cleaning the surface regularly will prevent the marker from adhering after long periods of time.

Climate Control

Summer Months

The summer months can be challenging to keep things running smoothly. There are several things that I would like to share with you to help get you through the heat of the summer.

Keeping windshield sun screens in the front cab of your vehicle will help keep the heat down inside your truck. If you have a pass-through door from your cab to your grooming area, your a/c will always be compromised by the cab heating up. Always crack the windows in the cab area so the heat will not build up.

If you have a generator that is mounted in a box, you may want to open the box door during hot summer days to let fresh air into the generator to prevent overheating. Just don't forget to close it before you leave your appointment.

Many vehicles have a passage door from the cab to the grooming area. It is next to impossible for dog hair not to get into the cab area. When using the air conditioning in the cab area, never turn it on the re-circulate setting. This feature allows the cool air in the cab to be re-circulated throughout the vehicle. This will draw dog hair through your a/c system, which can cause damage over time.

Grey tanks can develop a sour odor if they are not deodorized, especially during the hot summer months. You can use bleach to deodorize the grey tank. After emptying the tank, add a couple of gallons of fresh water and a cup of bleach, and let it sit for about 30 minutes, then drain. Taking a quick drive around the block will swoosh the water around. Vinegar is another form of deodorizer that you can use that is noncorrosive. I have also heard of using bromine, which is the same chemical that is used in hot tubs.

Vehicles that have the HV dryer located in the back may tend to blow at a higher temperature during the summer. The back of these vehicles will heat up due to the high temperature outside. In most vehicles the a/c has no way of reaching that area. The HV dryer is pulling hot air into the van and re-circulating it through the motor. It heats up very quickly and can become very uncomfortable for the dog. I open the back door to the vehicle while I am working to allow fresh air in, which will keep the HV dryer running at the proper temperature.

Winter Months

During the winter months when temperatures drop below 35 degrees, you must plug your shore line into your home in order to run space heaters when you are not working. This will prevent the plumbing in the vehicle from freezing. Over the years I have used a ceramic heater in the back of the van where the plumbing is located and also in the grooming area to regulate the proper temperature. I found that I was replacing ceramic heaters at least twice throughout the winter. This is because ceramic heaters run with a fan and heating coil. The fan pulls in dog hair, so these heaters quickly burn out. I started using an oil-filled heater many years ago. Because these heaters are filled with oil, there are no fans or electric coils to burn out. This type of heater will keep your van nice and warm throughout the night. Oil-filled space heaters run on a thermostat which you can set to whatever temperature you choose. I will use this heater during the day when it is extremely cold out while I am grooming. It does pull a lot of amps, so you must remember to turn it off when using dryers. This heater projects a nice natural, even heat that really warms you to the bone. I have a low-profile model which I prefer, as it stays put behind my grooming table without having to secure it in place.

You should always keep hot water heaters on during freezing temperatures. This will prevent them from freezing, which can cause extensive damage.

I like to keep my van toasty in the winter no matter what the temperature is outside. This way my products will stay at room temperature.

Driving a Trailer

Since I am now a proud owner of a grooming trailer, I thought I would share with you some tips and techniques that will help you when towing a mobile grooming trailer.

If you are not confident in backing into driveways, I would recommend parking on the street. If you have customers who live on busy streets, you may want to bring an orange cone with you and place it behind your trailer for safety.

Never pull straight into a driveway because backing out can be difficult, as trailers are very easy to jackknife.

When backing into a driveway it is always easier to back in with your driver's side on the same side of the street as your customer's house. It is much harder to back into a driveway with the passenger side on the same side of the street as the driveway.

When coming up to a driveway you want to swing close to the driveway entrance, then back over the center of the street, positioning the trailer to where it is on an angle ready to back into the driveway, as shown in this sequence of photos.

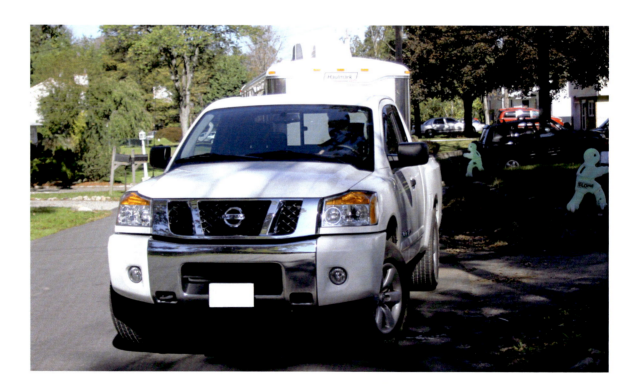

Once you position the trailer at an angle in front of the client's driveway, it will be easy to back in.

When backing up, look at the bottom of your steering wheel. If you want the trailer to go to the right, then move the bottom on the wheel to the right

If you want the trailer to go to the left, then move the bottom of the steering wheel to the left .

If you see that the trailer is starting to jackknife, you must stop and pull forward until the trailer straightens out. Back up slowly. If you back up too quickly you will get into trouble very fast.

My rule of thumb is, if it is going to take me longer to back into a driveway than it would to park on the street and walk to the front door, then I will park on the street and walk to the front door. Try not to waste valuable time.

Trailer Safety

The most important safety issue with a trailer is to always make sure you are properly hitched to your tow vehicle. Every morning check your hitch, covering these steps.

> Check to make sure your safety chains are properly connected.
> Check your connection for your lights. Make sure all lights are working properly.
> Check your trailer brakes, if applicable.
> Check to make sure your hitch is locked.
> Check to make sure your locking pin is properly in place.

Once you check your hitch, check it again! Dave has been in the tree business for many years and has seen so many tree chippers fall off vehicles due to negligence when hitching to their vehicle. Thank goodness he never lost one; however, he learned from everyone else's mistakes.

You should not take this safety inspection lightly. A trailer becoming unhitched on a busy road can result in tragedy.

Tip to Remember:

Always think safety first. When a client trusts you with their animal it is your responsibility to be sure the pet does not get injured. Keep your vehicle well maintained and carry spare parts in case of an emergency. The experiences that I have shared with you have all taught me valuable lessons. I hope these tips will prevent you from mishaps.

CHAPTER TWELVE

In and Out with Style

Mobile grooming is all about timing. Time is money. It is so important to get the dogs done in a timely fashion, yet with quality work.

Once I became established with my set clientele I very rarely would take on new customers. I do a lot of scissoring with very few shave-downs. All of my clients are on four to six week standing appointments. I have developed a very good reputation in town with my veterinarians. I am in and out of almost every appointment in one hour with very few exceptions.

It is very important to get the dogs on good schedules and to find the right trim for them. There is no time to de-mat at every stop and no time to reset overgrown patterns.

Groomers are creative people by nature. I know I enjoy making the dogs look like the breed they were bred to be. There is nothing attractive about a shave-down, although some people like it and that's fine. If you shave a dog down, you must remember that this dog most likely will not be back within four to six weeks. You may not see this dog again for three months. I do, however, have a few shave-downs that I see every five weeks. They are mostly 4F trims. Shaving down five weeks of growth is easy and can be done quickly.

The more stylish you keep your pet trims, the more frequently you will see that dog. It is challenging to put style in your grooms. Our objective as groomers should be to custom tailor our trims to bring out the best qualities in our pets as well to keep our trims practical and manageable for the pet owner.

There is nothing more rewarding than clients telling me that people on the street always ask them where they have their dog groomed. Many of my clients have told me that their vet has asked them who groomed their dog. I get such a charge out of that. It keeps me motivated to be the best groomer in town!

In order to get your clients on good schedules you can talk to them about the benefits of having their dog groomed regularly.

> You can discuss with them how regular bathing will promote healthy skin and coat. Share with them what products you use and how they are top quality and good for the skin and coat.

> Regular nail trims will eliminate splayed feet, which can contribute to arthritis later on in life. Regular trims will also keep the quick in the nail pushed back. As nails become overgrown the quick (vein) will grow to a length where you cannot get the nail cut back short enough without causing it to bleed.

> Trimming the pads of the feet prevents tracking in dirt and mud.

> Cleaning and plucking ears helps to keep ears healthy.

> Sanitary trims are done for cleanliness.

> Regular grooming prevents matting.

Finding the Right Trim and Schedule

The first thing I like to do when starting with a new client is look at the trim the dog is in. Is it flattering to the dog? Is it correct per the breed standard? Is there something that I can do to make the dog look cuter? I will talk to the client about the dog and make suggestions that I feel would benefit the dog.

When you prepare a dog properly, the trim will last longer for the client. When dogs come back in four to six weeks and you wash and dry them, they should look just like they did at the last appointment, just longer. That is when you know you have done a good job. If their coat looks very uneven, then you know you need to work on your preparation and scissor work.

Look at the dog's schedule. Is this a good grooming schedule for this breed? Is it a good schedule for the trim that you are doing? Cocker Spaniels, for example, are one breed that can be difficult to maintain unless you have them in nice short cute trims and they are on a four to five week grooming schedule.

If the client likes the trim and the dog is coming back matted, then you have to change the schedule and recommend the dog be on a five week schedule instead of a six week schedule (or whatever schedule you have; just bump it up a week). If the client does not want to change the dog's schedule, then you need to change the trim. Tell the client that you will tighten the trim to make it last a bit longer so you won't have any problems with matting. You can also spot condition. If you see that the dog is matting behind the ears or tail, you can condition those areas heavily.

Make sure you are not leaving too much hair in the wrong places, especially behind the ears of Bichons.

Look at the lifestyle of the client. Many breeds love to be in the water during the warm-weather months. Many people love to bring their dogs to the beach and even camping. You have to take all these things into consideration when putting trims on their dogs. In these situations I will tighten my trims for the warm-weather season. Leaving hair in the wrong places will only contribute to matting. You can add style to your trims by leaving hair in the right places and taking hair off in the right places.

I like to have summer trims, winter trims and vacation trims. I will change the trim a bit based on what is going on. During the winter months if we are getting a lot of snow and the dog's legs and feet are coming back matted I will tighten the trim up a little. If I know the clients are going out of town and the dog will be boarded, I will tighten the trim. If I am going away and I know the dog will have to wait a week longer than normal, I will tighten the trim. During the holiday rush I will tighten everyone just a bit in October/November so I am sure I will be able to get in and out of my stops quickly during the hectic month of December. All of these things go unnoticed by the clients. They never realize that I have done anything different. They trust me 100% and let me do whatever I feel fit. That's the great thing about this business, which you will see.

The bottom line is if the owner doesn't want to change the pet's grooming schedule to eliminate matting, then you must modify the trim. If the owner likes the trim just the way it is, you should recommend a more frequent schedule. You must do this to prevent you from de-matting at every visit. Maintenance is the key here; maintaining a good trim is my goal.

Adding style to your work is easier said than done. It takes an artistic eye. It also takes time, experience and practice to develop that artistry. It is very important for groomers to visit dog shows to see how these breeds should look as well as how the breeds are being stylized in the show ring. Just as our hairstyles are always changing, so are the breeds' styles. The show ring is where all the new trends are happening. Dog shows are fun to watch and you will most likely see breeds that you have never seen in person before. It is a great learning experience. Don't hesitate to talk to handlers when they are grooming and ask questions. As long as they are not rushing to get ringside they are usually very happy to chat.

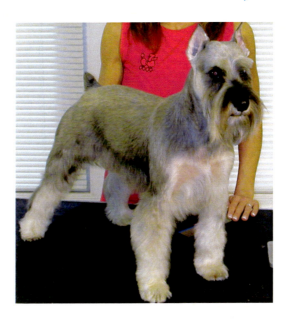

The most important thing that I have learned in the contest ring is to be methodical when I groom. Always start in the same place and end in the same place on every dog. If you tend to jump around, you will lose time. When you have a system when you groom you will become faster and the dogs will know what to expect every time. I remember when I was judging a grooming competition and was watching the groomers in the ring. I saw a girl jumping around the dog constantly. She had no system at all. She ran out of time during two of her competitions. After the second competition I told her what I saw and I explained to her that she needed to have a system. She did what I told her during her next class and she placed. She was so excited. It really makes a difference.

I remember the late, great Liz Paul told me years ago "tight body, big legs." This always stuck with me throughout the years. When you tighten the bodies and scissor the legs nice and full on the coated breeds, it really puts style on your dogs. Setting in rear angulation makes a huge difference in the dogs' appearance.

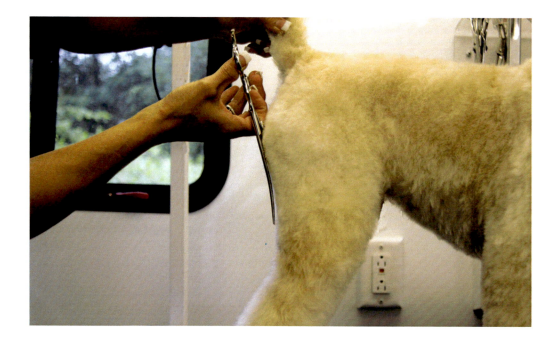

Almost all of my pet trims are done with nicely scissored legs. I always scissor the back of the front legs and also the inside and outside of the legs shorter and leave the front of the legs longer. This will give your dogs style without leaving too much coat.

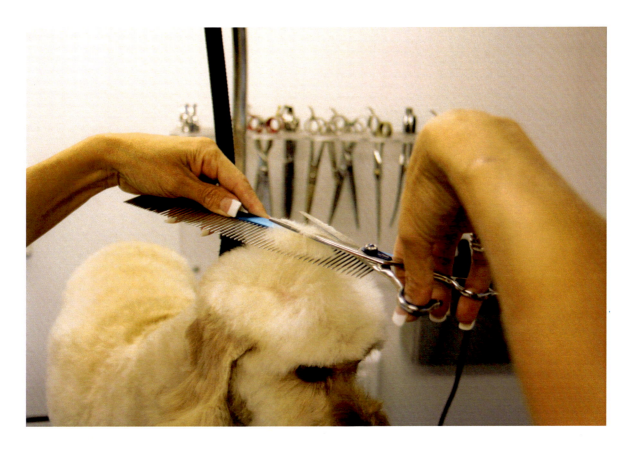

I use thinning shears on almost every dog that I groom. Thinners will give your grooms that finished look, eliminating scissor lines and clipper marks. I have a line of signature thinning shears that I put together to handle any coat type and texture.

Equipment

Everything from bathing systems, dryers, clippers, blades, brushes and scissors all play a major role in your efficiency. Investing in good equipment is vital in grooming. Bathing systems will save you time, shampoo and water and are worth every penny. I currently use the Prima Encore system which is great for the mobile vans. When using this system no pre-wetting or scrubbing coats is necessary due to the high pressure of the application. The freshly diluted shampoo mixture is sprayed directly onto the dry coat, which saves water and time from mixing shampoo. This is a portable system that can be easily installed into any grooming vehicle. It has a lot of power and really gets the dogs clean. It is especially beneficial to the heavier-coated dogs, as it penetrates the coats very quickly.

Keep your equipment sharp and in good repair. If you are fighting with faulty clippers, dull blades and dull scissors, you are wasting valuable time. Be sure you always have backup equipment in case you need it. I always carry at least three or four of each blade with me. I have several clippers, several combs and a huge variety of brushes. I have many shears as well. If you ever drop your shears by mistake, they may become nicked, so you will need a backup.

Quality shears will improve your grooming time. Shears can be expensive; however, they are one tool that will make or break your finished product. Shears are something that you really need to invest in. If you ever use a good quality shear, you will see the difference immediately in your work. Inexpensive shears will not do your work any justice. I remember when I was competing in the grooming competition ring, I had a separate tack box just for the ring. I had top quality shears and only used them in the contest ring. I had nice shears for my everyday work; however, my very expensive shears were for the contest ring. Once I retired from competing I still kept my shears separate. One day I was scissoring a standard poodle topknot and my hand was cramping up because the dog's coat was so thick. I grabbed my really good shears out of my bag and started to use them on the poodle. I couldn't believe how they just sliced through the coat like butter. All this time I thought they were too good to use every day and in turn I was cheating myself. Your work is only as good as the equipment that you are using, so save your money and invest in good equipment.

Quality dryers are very important. So many groomers ask me how I can get done within an hour at each appointment. I always ask, "What dryer do you have?" Nine times out of ten it is a dryer that does not have the force that is needed. A good quality high-velocity dryer will save you so much time. My favorite dryer is powered by two 22,500 rpm motors and has 58,329 fpm airflow. It has two speeds and is 17 amps, which come with the Wag'n Tails Pet Pro van. I believe that it makes a huge difference in your finished product when you use a stand dryer in addition to an HV dryer. It will improve your scissoring skills tremendously. When you scissor a coat that has wrinkles or waves it is difficult to get a nice finish on the coat. Every time you comb the coat the waves turn another way and your scissor work will fall apart. It is very difficult to get a nice finish on a dog that has waves in the coat. Stand dryers are also great for heads. Many dogs fuss about having their heads dried with an HV dryer, this is when a stand dryer comes in handy. It is also great for puppies.

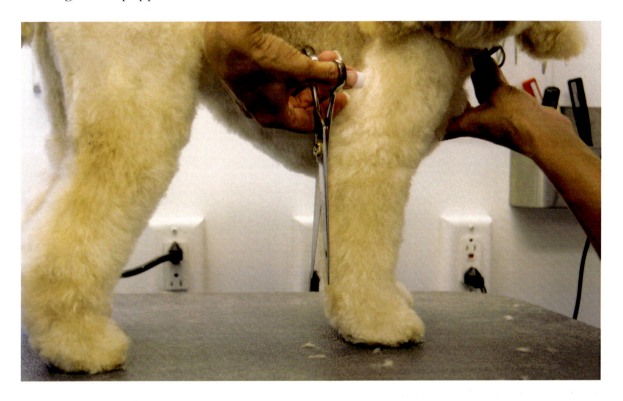

There are many benefits of using a Clippervac® system in a mobile unit. This system will eliminate excess hair in the small working environment of a mobile van, which also keeps the air quality clean, keeping your lungs healthy. If you find that you are having difficulty with finish work, this system will help you get to your finished product without excessive scissoring. The Clippervac® will help cut your grooming time down substantially. This system is an option that many grooming conversion companies offer.

A well built grooming table is very important, especially when working with larger breeds. Ultralift electric grooming tables are extremely sturdy and have the ability to lower to a comfortable height which allows the larger breeds to jump up on the table. It also will raise up to a height which makes it easy to work on smaller breeds. Working on a table that is either to low or to high can put stress on your back and shoulders over time. This table also has a slide out ramp which allows the dogs to walk over to the bath tub. Electric tables are highly recommended.

We sell our business as being convenient for our customers. When your grooming appointments become lengthy, you will lose money and your service becomes inconvenient. Having the right equipment will help you to be efficient.

Pre-Work

I learned early on by trial and error when to pre-clip and when not to. When you have breeds like Cocker Spaniels, Schnauzers, Poodles or any other breed that requires clipper work, I have found that if I pre-clip before the bath, it will save me a lot of drying time. I remember when I first started grooming I had a Cocker Spaniel that I just put right in the tub. It took me forever to get her face dried because first of all, I didn't have a stand dryer at the time and second, she hated the force dryer on her face. I learned very quickly to pre-clip faces before the bathtub so they can practically air dry on their own. I pre-clip back work, faces, ears on certain breeds and Poodle face/feet. I have even come across dogs that absolutely hate to be dried period, in this case I will do as much pre work as I can to eliminate excessive drying.

If I have a dog that I am going to shave down and it only has four to five weeks of growth, most of the time I will put it right in the tub. However, if I have a dog that has an inch or two of growth, I would shave them first. You don't want to waste shampoo and waste time drying hair that is only going to be shaved off.

These are the only situations where I pre-clip. Other than that, I prefer to put every dog straight in the tub. It is a good idea to keep your pre-clipping blades separate from your finish blades, since you are using them on dirty coats.

De-matting Techniques

Once you begin rebooking your clients you want to look at the condition of their dog's coat. Is the dog coming back matted? If the dog is matted, you want to look at several things.

> Look at your products. Are you using the right shampoo for that coat type? Are you using a deep cleansing shampoo without conditioning? Deep cleansers will strip the oils from the coat, which can dry the coat out. When the coat becomes dry it can mat easily. Conditioning every dog will prevent matting. The conditioner can be very diluted for Poodle-type coats or less diluted for drop silky coats. Deep cleansers are great for oily coats, but just be sure to add a bit of conditioner back into the coat.

Are you using the proper brushes and techniques? If you are using brushes that are very harsh, you may be damaging the coat. Damaged coat will mat very easily.

De-matting a coat incorrectly will cause damage and most likely cause the coat to mat up again. I prefer to de-mat in the tub when the dogs are wet and soapy. If you brush a dry dirty coat before the bath, you will brush dirt and debris through the hair shafts. This damages the coat severely. If you lather the coat up really well, then start brushing from the bottom of the mat up into the mat, it will slide apart. When the coat is wet and soapy the little barbs on the hair shaft will lie flat, which allows the strands of hair to slide apart. Hair is also more pliable when it is wet, so it will give. When hair is dry and you overstretch it with brushing, it can break and become damaged. When the coat is dry these little barbs are sticking out catching on to dirt and debris and tangling with the other barbed hair, which makes it difficult to brush out. De-matting solutions are available that help to release mats. If a dog is severely matted I will not de-mat the dog. I will brush out ears, tail and minor matting but no more than that. Severe de-matting is not fair to the dog. I would recommend shaving the dog down and starting over. At that time I would recommend the proper grooming schedule to keep the coat in better condition. When dogs are on schedules you will not see severe matting.

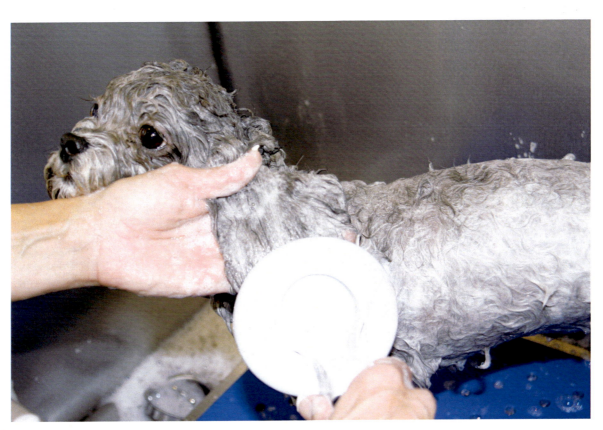

Look at your coat preparation. Are you getting the dogs completely dry? Leaving a coat damp will cause matting. Are you getting a brush and comb through the dog during your preparation? You never want to leave tangles in the coat. They will just become worse as the weeks go by, besides the fact that it is very unprofessional. Brushing through all the dogs with a heated dryer will stretch the coat out very straight and will dry the coat thoroughly.

De-shedding Techniques

I never brush a dirty coat, as discussed above, nor do I brush a double-coated breed before the bath. All my de-shedding gets done in the tub when the dogs are wet and soapy.

Several things trigger shedding, such as stress, temperature and illness. Have you ever noticed that when you bring a short-coated breed to the vet, or get them in your grooming van, they will shed like crazy? Stress will release coat. Most importantly, temperature releases coat. During the winter dogs tend to hang on to their coat, where during the warmer months they release coat. When you bathe dogs in warm water the follicles will dilate and the coat will release. This is the best time to shed these breeds out. Brush the coat when it is wet and soapy and all the dead undercoat will just flow out.

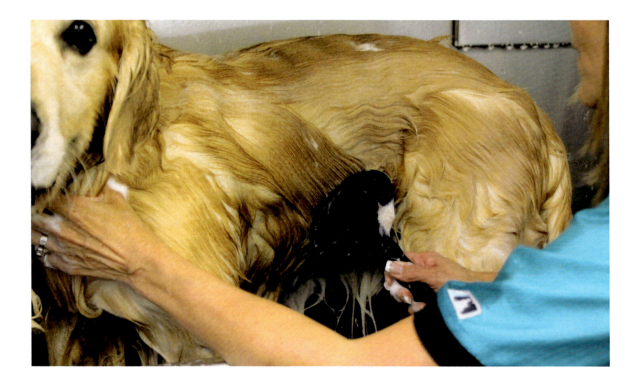

Make sure you keep the dog very soapy during brushing. The water flow on the dog while brushing at the same time will also keep the coat coming out. By doing this I feel that we are taking advantage of coat that may not have been ready to come out for a week or so because of the fact that we are brushing it out while the follicles are dilated. This keeps the shedding down to a minimal for clients.

Be careful when you are brushing a wet coat. The brush will reach the skin more quickly than when the coat is dry. Always watch for irritation. If you feel you are irritating the skin, you need to stop. Make sure your brush is not too harsh on the skin. For example, I always brush the rear furnishings on Golden Retrievers over my hand so I am brushing on my hand and not against their skin. You also want to brush tails the same way, over your hand.

After I feel that I have removed as much undercoat as possible I will give the dog a cool rinse. This will help constrict the follicles.

When you high-velocity dry these breeds you will see that you will hardly have any hair blowing around your vehicle, which is a healthier environment for you. You will also notice that the dogs will dry very quickly. Undercoat has a thicker shaft of hair that absorbs moisture. It takes longer to dry than guard hair. When you remove all the undercoat in the tub you will have a huge mound of wet soapy hair. Keep in mind that dogs that have not had this done before may take more than one visit to remove all the undercoat. Always keep an eye on the skin for irritation. If the skin becomes pink, you want to stop brushing.

Tip to Remember:

Your equipment plays a vital role in your efficiency. Investing in good quality equipment is important. Have a system when you groom and groom that way with every dog. The more consistent you are the more efficient you will become. Continuing education should be a part of your career as a professional pet stylist. Attending seminars annually will help you fine tune your skill level. The more educated you are the more successful you will become. Take pride in your work and your business will blossom.

CHAPTER THIRTEEN

Expanding Your Business

Adding Another Vehicle

Most mobile groomers go through a phase where they are very busy and are turning customers away on a daily basis, so they start to think about putting another vehicle on the road to make more money. It is a nice thought, that's for sure. I am guilty of it myself. Before you decide whether you want to jump into buying another vehicle and hiring a groomer, you have to ask yourself a few questions first.

- Why did you decide to go mobile in the first place? What was so attractive about mobile grooming?
- Do you want to be responsible for an employee and another vehicle?

It is very enjoyable to work for yourself and make your own hours. Do you want the responsibility of another vehicle on the road? Do you want to be responsible for another groomer? What if this person's quality of work is not as good as yours? Will that bother you? Do you want to be responsible for routing yourself and another groomer? These are all things you have to think long and hard about.

If this sounds good, then go for it! Many groomers out there have put multiple vehicles on the road.

Hiring a Groomer

If you are not sure if you want to go this route, you can always hire someone part-time and let her or him work your van on your days off. This will give you a taste of whether being a boss is going to work for you and will also give you an opportunity to see if this potential employee is responsible enough to work a second vehicle for you.

You may even want to hire someone to do the bath dogs that you may not want to do. You can train someone to be a bather/brusher. Teach this person to trim furnishings and feet and tidy up those double coats.

If you can find someone you can rely on and feel comfortable with, then it will be a great business decision. Most groomers pay the employees a commission. You would be responsible for the van and the overhead, including the gas your employee uses. The commission will depend on your expenses and what you can afford to pay. Some groomers pay 40% and I have seen some pay 60%. You will have to analyze your situation and see what works best for you. Growing your business by adding on vehicles can be very profitable, although it brings on more responsibility.

Hiring an Assistant

Many mobile groomers have assistants work with them. The assistants can be paid a daily rate or an hourly rate. I have hired assistants during the summer months. I have had high-school kids ask to work with me, which actually worked out nicely. I would pay them a daily rate. They would do all my bathing/drying for me. During that time I could return calls and catch up on paperwork. On days when we had larger dogs I would bring a second HV dryer with me so we could team up and get the dog dried faster. When we had multiple pets in one household, having as assistant was really great. She would wash the first dog, I would start drying and then she would wash and dry the second dog while I started grooming.

While I was finishing up grooming, my assistant would write out my invoices and clean up the van. When I took the dogs into the client's home, my assistant would do a complete clean-up and make sure everything was tied down, so when I got back in the van I was ready to roll. I enjoyed having the company and it really made the day go by fast. Even if you had only a part-time assistant, that would allow you to book your multiple pet homes on days when you had help.

Tip to Remember:

Expanding your business is a sign of success. Before taking the next step make sure that this is the path you want to take. When hiring an employee, a new set of policies and procedures should be put in place for your employee. Consult with your accountant and insurance agency regarding hiring employees.

CHAPTER FOURTEEN

Continuing Education

Trade Shows

Trade shows are held all over the United States. It is very beneficial to attend these shows. You will meet so many groomers you can network with and develop camaraderie with. It will really keep you connected with what is going on in the industry. There is so much to learn. We never stop learning as groomers. If you go to a trade show and pick up one piece of information, it was worth the trip. Keeping your skills up and learning new techniques will keep your business blossoming.

You will enjoy shopping at all the different vendors and being able to see all the new products and equipment that are available to you. There are always show specials you can take advantage of to purchase supplies. Contact show managers to be put on their mailing list so you can be sure to receive upcoming show information.

Instructional DVDs

I have the most complete instructional DVD series available. This series includes the most popular breed trims, mixed breed trims and technique DVDs that will help advance your skill levels.

De-shedding and de-matting techniques, as discussed in the Chapter 12 In and Out with Style, are also on DVD if you would like to see how it is done up close and personal. You can visit my website, www.jodimurphy.net, for a complete list of DVDs and watch video clips online.

Available on DVD at www.jodimurphy.net:

Volume 1: Scissoring: Theory & Techniques
Volume 2: Thinning Shears: Theory & Techniques
Volume 3: Before The Groom
Volume 4: On The Same Page: One on One With A Veterinarian
Volume 5: Smooth Road to Shavedowns
Volume 6: De-shedding: Theory & Techniques
Volume 7: Airedale Terrier
Volume 8: West Highland White Terrier
Volume 9: American Cocker Spaniel Pet Trims
Volume 10: Maltese
Volume 11: Golden Retriever
Volume 12: Miniature Schnauzer
Volume 13: Poodle
Volume 14: Shih Tzu
Volume 15: Lhasa Apso
Volume 16: Irish Setter
Volume 17: Yorkshire Terrier
Volume 18: Soft Coated Wheaten Terrier Pet Trim
Volume 19: Welsh Terrier
Volume 20: Bichon Frise Pet Trim
Volume 21: Puppy Cut
Volume 22: Goldendoodle
Volume 23: Cockapoo
Volume 24: Portuguese Water Dog: A Poodle in Disguise
Volume 25: American Cocker Spaniel Show Trim
Volume 26: Bichon Frise Show Trim
Volume 27: Soft Coated Wheaten Show Trim
Volume 28: Border Terrier
Volume 29: De-Matting: Theory & Technique
Volume 30: Scottish Terrier
Volume 31: Snap On Combs: Theory & Techniques
Volume 32: Carding & Handstripping for Pets
Volume 33: Havanese

Volume 34: Secrets of the Contest Ring
Volume 35: Fragile: Handle with Care

Mobile Grooming I: The Business End
Mobile Grooming II: A Day in the Spa

Certification Organizations

You can become a member of several certification organizations. They offer member discounts to shows, among many other perks. Becoming a member allows you to receive newsletters throughout the year to keep you up on what is going on in the industry.

If you choose to become a Certified groomer, these organizations will help guide you. Certification really helps you to understand the breeds, not only the grooming but also the history, the origin and the utility of the breeds. This will help you understand temperaments and why dogs act the way they do sometimes. Knowing and understanding breeds will help you educate your clients. I have had so many clients over the years ask me what type of dog they should add to their family. Knowing the type of family they are, whether they have small children and other relevant factors will help you guide them in choosing the right breed.

If Mrs. Smith has a Westie that keeps digging in her yard, chasing squirrels and running from her and she can't understand why, you will know what to say if you understand terriers and what they were bred for. If Mrs. Jones has little kids and she has a shelty that keeps chasing the kids while nipping at their heels, you will be able to explain to her that her shelty is a herding dog and that's what shelties were bred to do, herd sheep (not children; however, they don't know the difference). Certification is a personal choice. The more educated you are the more valuable you will be to your clients. Becoming a member shows your customers that you are connected and take your profession seriously.

> National Dog Groomers of America
> International Pet Groomers
> International Society of Canine Cosmetology

Many resources are available to help you stay on top of your game in this industry.

Tip to Remember:

The more you know the further you will go. You hold the key to your own success.

A Few Words From Fellow Mobile Groomers Around the Country…

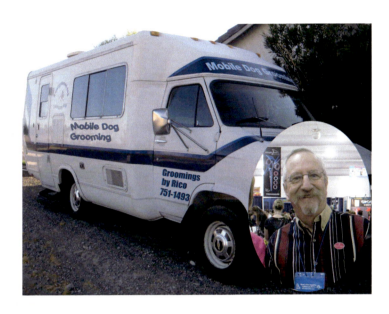

You hear it all the time: Mobile Grooming is not for everybody. It's true that some groomers love it and others don't, but I've found that most in the last group never had the proper training. Mobile grooming presents a series of challenges that the store groomer can't even fathom and it will take years to figure it all out by yourself.

I was approaching my sixties when I thought of dog grooming as a viable post-retirement career. I wished I would have started ten years earlier, so by the time I finally left my desk job I could have been (with any luck) half as good as the groomers I saw in the grooming magazines.

I came across Jodi Murphy's Mobile Grooming DVD (A Day in the Spa) and I ordered it with great curiosity. Boy, was I in for a treat! I (virtually) rode with Jodi in her van for 5 hours, she became my mentor and my friend and I saw firsthand the inside of that mysterious "mobile grooming business". I liked what I saw: People coming out of their houses to greet you, dogs being groomed pretty much in their own environment and sunlight (and some rain too) all around you! Oh, and the profitability was not bad either.

A few short months after that, my first grooming van was ready and my DVDs were almost worn out, however by the time I hit the road for the first time, I felt ready! Now, I won't lie and say that I became half as good as Jodi Murphy (I'm only human…), but I was well prepared, organized and knowledgeable enough to go through the process with minimal surprises.

I still review those DVD's every now and then. A little because they nostalgically remind me of the beginnings of my final career but mainly because I keep learning little details here and there, nuances that I failed to catch even the last go around. Jodi's knowledge and experience are so vast that I don't see them running out soon!

I continue my education with Jodi's Instructional Series. A customer recently told me: "We've been all over the country (he's a long haul driver). No groomer has ever done Mini the way you do!" Well, duh! I may take credit for not cutting the little guy, everything else comes straight out of Jodi's Maltese DVD.

Whether in person, on a DVD or though her writings, Jodi Murphy has an uncanny ability to communicate her knowledge. Most likely because she is genuinely happy to share with us her expertise and her non pretentious, friendly and down-to-earth way of teaching resonates with everybody. This book will not be different!

Ricardo Rocha
Pahrump, NV

Going Mobile was the best move I could have ever made! After owning a shop for over 8 yrs, I could never go back. Mobile has given me a Family life again. I work when I want to, Vacation when I feel I need it and no one has to know. I can pick and choose my clients too. My clients are more like family and I know them all on a first name basis. My tips are overwhelming and I make more money now than owning a shop. I love being Mobile and my Freedom.

Marilyn Wainright
A Purr-Fect Paw Mobile Pet Grooming
Barnegat, NJ

Photo by Macy Pate

How do I love Mobile Grooming???? Let me count the ways! But the challenge will be to do it in 200 words or so….. What I love most is the independence of being my own boss. I love never missing a school function, and raising my children in the van. I look a little funny in the car rider line but my kids never complained. When I needed to go to grooming competitions I just rearranged my schedule. I can make as much money as I want. I love grooming a couple of dogs, rolling the windows down, turning the radio up, and cruising to my next stop with the wind blowing in my hair. Everyone is glad to see you and they appreciate the service and the relationship I have with their beloved pets. No ringing phones, no barking dogs, no drama, no unexpected drop-ins, or added dogs because someone called in sick. I started my grooming business in a homemade 1975 Ford RV. Now I drive a 2006 Wag'n Tail's Pet Pro van. I work about 3 days a week. I'm booked a year in advance and all dogs are groomed at least every 6 weeks so I know exactly what I can expect to find when I arrive! Life is GOOD!

Judy D. Hudson, NCMG
Groomingtails
Pet Tech Instructor CPR and Pet First Aid
Kingston Springs, TN

Being talked into going mobile was the best thing that could have ever happened! I love the freedom that I have. If I decide to take a day off I can I don't have to worry about a store front where people just stop in to make an appointment or for a nail trim. I don't miss having to have four or five dogs done within a short time span, working on one dog at a time gives me a chance to really spend time on their groom, but time to love on them as well. The dogs behave better, there is less stress.

I think what I love best of all is that I don't need to do as many dogs as I used to have to do to make a good pay check! By doing less dogs, I save my body from breaking down and from burnout. Having my weekends free is another huge plus!

Lisa Leady, NCMG
Primp My Pooch
Genoa, IL

I am a people's person. I love talking and making friends and I also love dogs. Being a Mobile groomer I can have both. I have customers I can call my friends, the relationship grows with every visit, I've seen their kids grow. I also groom some dogs I just adore. Some of them I've been grooming since their first groom and we celebrate every birthday. It brings great satisfaction knowing I can help my friends take care of their pets. Some of them cannot drive anymore and/or have too many dogs to drive to the closest shop. Being mobile just gives me the opportunity to provide them with an option. At the same time I had the opportunity to touch some of the owners lives, but most of all, I've been touch by them. Like the little dog that licks your face after you free him from his hairy jail, or the woman who enjoys your visits so much that is willing to keep her appointments even after her pooch has die. There are so many blessings I have received just by being mobile, so many people to reach, old dogs to groom, the joy they express when they see you at the door, the pride they show after been pampered, all just in their own front yard.

Juan Santiago
Da groomer mobile pet spa
Kissimmee, Fl, USA

I have been a mobile groomer for 7 yrs and have owned my own business, Calling All Dogs, for 5 yrs. I became a mobile groomer after spending 2 yrs in a grooming shop and not enjoying the assembly line of dogs and cats that were coming through the shop. I wanted a more personal experience with the animals and their owners. After attending a mobile grooming seminar in Hershey Pennsylvania, I knew this was for me. After just 6 months out on my own I couldn't take anymore clients. After one year, I decided to get another van and hire a groomer to cover all the calls. My groomer stayed on with me for 3 yrs. It was a wonderful experience. After she left, I couldn't find another groomer that fit my business so I sold the van, bought myself my first new van, Hanvey Sprinter, downsized my business to a 5 mile radius from my house. I do not have graphics on this van because I haven't been able to take on a new client in 2 yrs. There is so much freedom in mobile grooming. I love mobile grooming and still do as much as I did when I started.

Renee Christensen
Calling All Dogs
Long Island, NY

I started mobile grooming in 2001 after the veterinarian I worked for retired. My good friend Judy Hudson coached me through the whole process. She had been mobile for several years and had converted a couple of vans and motor homes into mobile units.

I bought my 19.5 ft. Coachman motor home from my in-laws and my husband and I converted it! I have found such freedom in making my own schedule, selecting my dogs and mapping out my route! The fact that I can do fewer dogs for more money is a tremendous bonus in going mobile.

In the beginning, when my son was younger, I would start early and be finished by the time he was out of school. Sometimes I would pick him up in what we lovingly refer to as "The Routley Limo!" My husband, Terry, is a director of a private school in our area so I was also able to work around his and Tyler's school breaks.

The client relationship becomes very personal and you really feel like a part of many of their families. I have seen their children grow up and been there when their pets have passed away and they have done the same with me. Starting out, I never imagined how fulfilling this type of grooming career was truly going to be.

Judy Routley
Little Judy's Roman Bath
Cooper City, FL
Certified Pet Tech Instructor
Oster Professional Products Ambassador

I started grooming pets when I was thirteen years old, I must say that was a long time ago. I have worked for veterinarians, kennels, pet stores, breeders and some grooming shops but I have to share with you my favorite of all is being mobile and working for myself.

The freedom that being mobile gives me has allowed me to enjoy my job even more. I have a grooming shop also, but will admit to you I am never there. The barking dogs, ringing phone and the constant "Is my dog done yet?!" drove me away from being a happy shop owner.

I added mobile services on in 2006 and started it slow, juggling the shop and a few days on the road. As I went along some of my shop clients decided to try the mobile out and I also got a lot of new clients. I then started going to my shop just one day a week and grooming in the mobile five days a week. I now do not go into my shop at all except to make sure it's still standing.

Being able to pick the areas that I want to work, the pets that I want to groom and how fast or slow I want my day to go is great. I feel less pressured and can enjoy my days more. Don't get me wrong there are pitfalls with being mobile. If something goes wrong with my truck or trailer, when gas prices go up and down, bad weather and road work, although I always say a bad day on the road is better than a good day in the shop!

My mobile clients appreciate me more than my shop clients ever did. Funny thing, about ten years ago I said I would never go mobile…. now I am never looking back.

Michelle Rizzi
Paws Fur Beauty
Roxbury, NJ

Certification Organizations

National Dog Groomers Association of America, Inc.
P.O. Box 101
Clark, PA 16113
Phone: 724-962-2711, FAX: 724-962-1919
www.ndgaa.com
ndga@nationaldoggroomers.com

International Society of Canine Cosmetologists
Pam Lauritzen, President
2702 Covington Dr
Garland, TX 75040
(972) 414-9715
iscc@petstylist.com

IPG
6475 Wallace Rd NW
Salem, OR 97304
503-551-2397
www.IPGICMG.com
Concepts@aol.com or Hayley@IPGICMG.com
Hayley Keyes 336-852-9867 or 336-340-7915

Trade Shows

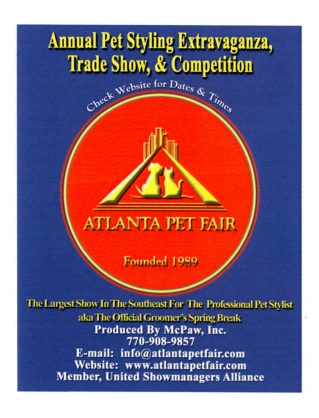

The Meadowlands Exposition Center
Secaucus, New Jersey 07094
Phone: 781-326-3376,
FAX: 781-326-2971
www.intergroom.com

40th All American Grooming Show
August 9 – 12, 2012
847-364-4547
Fax 847-364-0690
aagrmgshow@wowway.com
www.aagrmgshow.com

Groomer SuperShow at SuperZoo
800-999-7295 x 138 or 626-447-2222
www.superzoo.org
Mandalay Bay Convention Center, Las Vegas, NV
Sept.11-13, 2012/ July 23-25, 2013/July 22-24,
2014/July21-23, 2015

World Pet Association, Inc.
135 West Lemon Ave, Monrovia, CA 91016
www.worldpetassociation.org

New England Pet Grooming Professionals, Inc.
(One of the only non profit pet grooming associations in the USA)
Mission statement: Dedicated with Integrity to good health and beauty thru Kindness and Skill
web: www.NEPGP.com
Facebook: newenglandpetgroomingprofessionals
Phone: 508-799-5236 Toni Coppola, President
Email: lindacc@nepgp.com, or info@nepgp.com
Events: NEPGP SummerFest -July 13-15th, 2012 @ the Crowne Plaza in Warwick, RI 02886
Trade show, three divisions grooming competitions (including GroomTeam Sanctioned Open), educational seminars with nationally know speakers
NEPGP Fall Fling-a day long educational event held in the first week of November

U.S. Pet Pro Classic
Pam Lauritzen, Show Producer
2702 Covington Dr., Garland, TX 75040
(972) 414-9715
classic@petstylist.com

National Dog Groomers Association
of America, Inc.
P.O. Box 101, Clark, PA 16113
Phone: 724-962-2711, FAX: 724-962-1919
www.ndgaa.com
ndga@nationaldoggroomers.com

Colorado GroomFest – Denver, Co
June 8, 9 & 10, 2012
Fun In The Sun – Orlando, FL
Oct. 26, 27 & 28, 2012

Recommended Products and Suppliers

I wanted to share with you all my favorite reputable companies that I have come to trust and love throughout my career. I only recommend products and suppliers that I have used myself. These companies and manufacturers are highly respected in the grooming industry. They provide exceptional customer service and stand behind their products.

Products and Supplies 153

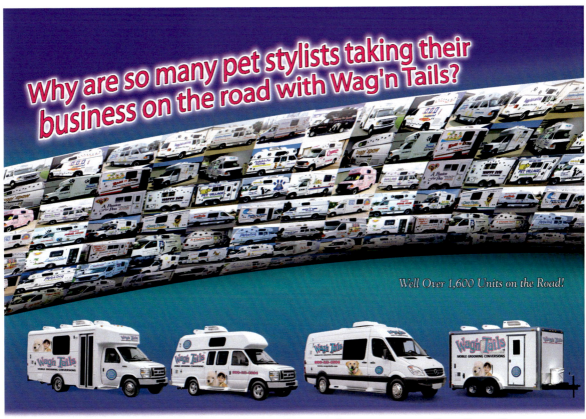

Well Over 1,600 Units on the Road!

They love the lifestyle. They trust the leader.

Mobile grooming is the best thing that's happened to the industry since the electric clipper. Groomers the world over are enjoying the pace and freedom of going mobile. Easier on you, easier on the customer, and better for the pets, mobile grooming combines profit with compassion and service.

Thinking about going mobile?

Talk to our customers. They'll never look back from the best decision they ever made. And Wag'n Tails makes everything easy, from helping you plan your business to easy financing to a full-time service manager who can hit any curve ball you can throw him.

Did we mention our exclusive 5-year 60,000 mile warranty? Our units aren't just the prettiest, they're the toughest, and we stand behind them like no one else. It's just one more reason to let us help you put your dreams in motion.

BEST BUILT 5-Year 60,000 Mile Warranty BEST BACKED

Put Your Dreams in Motion

Wag'n Tails
MOBILE GROOMING CONVERSIONS

Call Wag'n Tails at 800.513.0304 today or visit us on the web at www.wagntails.com to complete your no-obligation credit application.

Cleaner coats in less time.

The Prima ENCORE provides all the advantages of the well-known Prima Bathing System in a smaller, faster and easier to use new model. The portable ENCORE is configured for mobile and small salon groomers with limited operating space. The pump and interchangeable fluid containers can be customized to fit any location.

Groomers who use the Prima proclaim it is the most valuable tool in their shop. This environmentally friendly system delivers fresh shampoo quickly and effortlessly throughout the animal's coat. Prima's high pressure massages deep down to the skin for maximum cleaning efficiency. There is no pre-wetting or scrubbing and no wasted shampoo going down the drain.

You'll enjoy the savings of time, energy and money while pets love the deep cleaning scrubbing action. With the Prima ENCORE you will achieve happier customers, lower costs and higher profits.

www.primabathing.com
866-889-0877

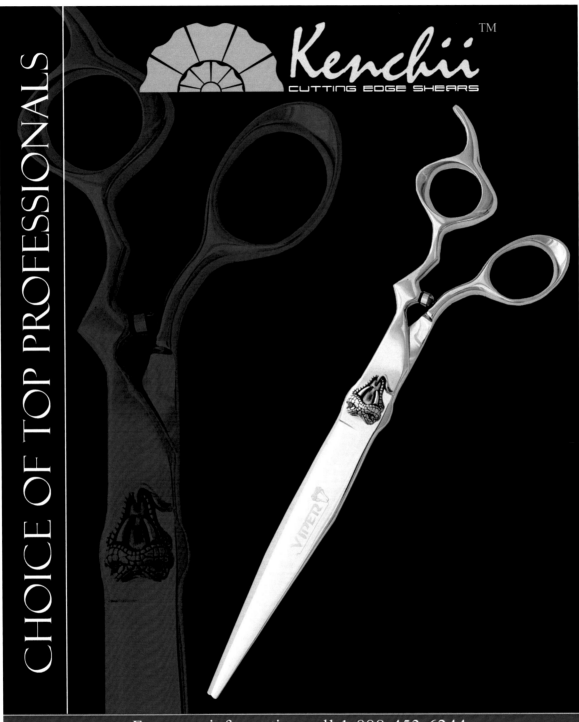